CONTRIBUTORY NEGLIGENCE

CONTRIBUTORY NEGLIGENCE

Principles and Practice

James Goudkamp
Donal Nolan

OXFORD
UNIVERSITY PRESS

OXFORD
UNIVERSITY PRESS

Great Clarendon Street, Oxford, OX2 6DP,
United Kingdom

Oxford University Press is a department of the University of Oxford.
It furthers the University's objective of excellence in research, scholarship,
and education by publishing worldwide. Oxford is a registered trade mark of
Oxford University Press in the UK and in certain other countries

First Edition published in 2018

Impression: 1

Published in the United States of America by Oxford University Press
198 Madison Avenue, New York, NY 10016, United States of America

British Library Cataloguing in Publication Data
Data available

Library of Congress Control Number: 2018949658

ISBN 978–0–19–881423–8

Printed and bound by
CPI Group (UK) Ltd, Croydon, CR0 4YY

FOREWORD

One of the most important areas of legal practice is the law of negligence. Since claims in negligence – especially personal injury claims – are commonly met by defences of contributory negligence, judges and practitioners have to apply that doctrine day in and day out. In doing so, they are liable to encounter a number of difficulties.

Some of these difficulties concern questions of law. To give only a few examples, to what causes of action, other than tortious negligence, does the doctrine of contributory negligence apply? Does it apply in cases of strict liability? Is the test of contributory negligence always objective, or can it sometimes take account of the characteristics of the individual claimant? If the claimant deliberately fails to take reasonable care for his own safety, can he be described as negligent? Is it relevant that the claimant failed to take reasonable care for his own safety, if the risk to which he negligently exposed himself was not a cause of the injuries which he sustained? In what circumstances can a claimant be contributorily negligent by reason of another person's conduct? How does contributory negligence operate in a situation where the damages recoverable by the claimant are also limited by the principle in *SAAMCO* (*South Australia Asset Management Corp v York Montague Ltd* [1997] AC 191)? If contributory negligence is pleaded along with other defences, such as *volenti non fit injuria* (that the claimant voluntarily incurred the risk of injury) or *ex turpi causa non oritur actio* (illegality), how do these defences interact with one another?

Other difficulties, arising in most if not all cases of contributory negligence, concern the apportionment of responsibility between the claimant and the defendant. As judges have often remarked, this naturally depends on the circumstances of the particular case. Nevertheless, it is important that the courts should adopt a coherent approach. It is elementary justice that like cases should be treated alike, and that unlike cases should be treated differently. But consistency is only possible if the courts are provided with information about apportionments in other comparable cases, and about the salient facts of those cases. The same requirement exists when practitioners seek to settle claims by agreement: the procedure by which the great majority of claims are determined.

The present work is designed to assist practitioners and the courts to address these difficulties. Parts I and II explain, clearly and succinctly, the law relating to contributory negligence. They answer all the questions mentioned above, and many others besides. Part III contains a guide to the practice of the UK courts in relation to apportionment in the factual situations which arise most commonly in practice. In relation to each of the most common categories of case – for example, cases where child pedestrians have been knocked down by motorists, or cases where the claimant failed to wear a seatbelt – statistics are given for the extent to which damages were discounted for contributory negligence, based on an analysis of all the cases decided by the courts during the past 20 years, so far as available. What emerges from these analyses is that the discounts applied by judges, in situations which arise time and time again, generally fall within a relatively narrow range. It is therefore possible to provide practice-based guidance as to the average extent to which damages are discounted in each category of case, and the general range of discounts, together with illustrations of circumstances involving a higher, or lower, discount than the average.

This concise book is the first guide since Glanville Williams's *Joint Torts and Contributory Negligence* (1951), published shortly after the passing of the Law Reform (Contributory Negligence) Act 1945 and the Law Reform (Miscellaneous Provisions) Act (Northern Ireland) 1948, both to the interpretation and effect of the legislation, and to how it is applied in practice by the courts of England and Wales, Scotland and Northern Ireland. It will assist courts and practitioners in understanding this area of the law, and in applying a consistent approach when assessing, in the most common types of case, the extent to which damages should be reduced for contributory negligence. It is greatly to be welcomed.

The Rt Hon Lord Reed
31 August 2018

PREFACE

We were inspired to write this book, and its forthcoming and more detailed companion volume, *Contributory Negligence in the Twenty-First Century* (OUP forthcoming), by a belief that considerable scope exists for original study regarding how tort law works 'in action', and that the relatively recent widespread online availability of judicial decisions has created the conditions for a new kind of legal scholarship that focuses not so much on individual decisions of high precedential value as on run-of-the-mill decisions. For several reasons, the law of contributory negligence struck us as an eminently suitable subject for exploration in this way. These reasons included the fact that the contributory negligence doctrine is very regularly in issue before the courts (meaning that we were assured of having a large sample of cases with which to work), and that it is usually possibly to see, at a glance, how courts determine the issue of contributory negligence (meaning that it is relatively easy to gather key data from the universe of decisions). We were also inspired in writing this volume by the desire to provide legal practitioners with a 'one-stop-shop' where they could find a concise and accurate statement of the legal principles governing contributory negligence alongside an empirically informed analysis of the way that the doctrine operates in various recurrent scenarios.

Parts of this book were presented at the Personal Injuries Bar Association's Annual Conference 2017 and the Professional Negligence Bar Association's Liability Day 2017. We are indebted to the participants in those events for their constructive feedback. We are also grateful for the indispensable research assistance and statistical support that we received in connection with this project from Mercy Akoth, Charles Austin, Eleni Katsampouka, Lindsay Lee, and Mengfei Ying. Oxford University Press provided valuable input throughout the production process, and we were also assisted by the thoughtful comments of the referees who reviewed our publication proposal. In addition, we wish to acknowledge the support provided by the excellent librarians in the Bodleian Law Library, especially Elizabeth Wells, who helped us to track down several sources that otherwise would have eluded us, and to thank Lord Reed for generously agreeing to write the foreword. Finally, the University of Oxford Law Faculty and the John Fell Oxford University Press Research Fund provided us with vital financial support in connection with this project over the course of several years, for which we are most grateful. It is no exaggeration to say that the project simply would not have been possible without it.

James Goudkamp
Donal Nolan
16 April 2018
Oxford

CONTENTS

TABLE OF CASES

AUSTRALIA

CANADA

IRELAND

NEW ZEALAND

UNITED KINGDOM

TABLE OF LEGISLATION

Part I

1

INTRODUCTION

(1) The Law of Contributory Negligence

Contributory negligence is a failure by a claimant to take reasonable care for his or her own safety or interests that is causally related to the damage about which he or she complains. At common law, a finding of contributory negligence defeated actions to which the contributory negligence doctrine applied. However, since 1945 (in England, Wales, and Scotland[1]) and 1948 (in Northern Ireland[2]), legislation has provided that contributory negligence does not prevent liability from arising but that the damages shall instead be reduced according to the parties' respective shares of responsibility.[3] Although these statutes were enacted long ago, and despite the fact that they have been applied by the courts on countless occasions,[4] there has never been a systematic attempt in the United Kingdom (or in any of the many other jurisdictions where similar legislation has been enacted) to determine empirically how the courts apply the law of contributory negligence. 1.01

(2) The Mischief Addressed

Williams's treatise. In 1951, at the dawn of the age of apportionment, Glanville Williams published his towering work *Joint Torts and Contributory Negligence*.[5] That book remains by a significant margin the most important contribution to this field of enquiry in any jurisdiction.[6] Williams realized that a full 1.02

[1] Law Reform (Contributory Negligence) Act 1945.

[2] Law Reform (Miscellaneous Provisions) Act (Northern Ireland) 1948.

[3] Similar legislation concerning collisions between ships had existed since 1911. See 3.09.

[4] Cases requiring the courts to apply the apportionment statutes 'are the regular diet of judges in the courts day in and day out': *St George v Home Office* [2008] EWCA Civ 1068, [2009] 1 WLR 1670 [54] (Dyson LJ).

[5] Glanville Williams, *Joint Torts and Contributory Negligence: A Study of Concurrent Fault in Great Britain, Ireland and the Common-Law Dominions* (Stevens & Sons 1951).

[6] 'Glanville Williams['s] ... text on contributory negligence ... remains, arguably, the best analysis available today' of the law in this area: *Chae v Min* [2001] ABQB 1071, (2001) 100 Alta LR (3d) 65 [14] (Veit J).

understanding of the law of contributory negligence requires ascertaining how the courts apply it in practice. He therefore compiled a short list of discounts that had been imposed under the then novel apportionment regime.[7] However, the novelty of apportionment meant that Williams had virtually no data with which to work. Furthermore, the interpretation of the legislation was then rather unsettled in important respects, with it having been said that the courts were at the time 'feeling [their] way in difficult country',[8] which meant that there was reason to doubt the consistency with which the legislation was being applied. The scanty materials on which Williams was able to draw, coupled with the fact that his analysis is now very dated, mean his work is of limited usefulness when it comes to understanding how judges apply the law of contributory negligence in the twenty-first century.

1.03 **The principle of consistent treatment.** It is important to understand how the contributory negligence doctrine operates in practice for two main reasons. The first of these reasons concerns the principle of consistent treatment. It is a fundamental principle of justice that like cases should be treated alike and that different cases should be treated differently. There is a distinct danger that this principle will not be observed as closely as it should be in relation to (in particular) the way in which damages are discounted for contributory negligence unless sufficient information as to the apportionment exercise is readily to hand. In the absence of adequate information in this connection, very different discounts may be imposed in materially equivalent cases and similar discounts in cases that are different from each other in relevant respects. Such outcomes are unjust and, thus, tend to bring the law into disrepute. One practitioner describes the problem as follows:[9]

> Deductions for contributory negligence seem to vary to an extent that often gives the impression that the level of deduction is totally arbitrary. That should not be the case. I believe that the problem often stems from advocates simply not assisting the court to reach the correct level of reduction, if any, by producing the relevant authorities to ensure that the judge does not go wrong.

By significantly increasing the amount of information that is conveniently available about how judges apply the law of contributory negligence, and especially about how they discount damages, this volume aims to reduce the risk of injustice in this regard.

1.04 **Facilitating settlement.** The other reason why it is important to understand how the contributory negligence doctrine operates in practice is that this should promote the settlement of disputes in which contributory negligence is an issue. For example, our study reveals that, in certain recurrent situations, judges tend to opt for discounts that fall within a relatively small range. In such situations, actual

[7] Williams (n 5) 391.

[8] *Jones v Livox Quarries Ltd* [1952] 2 QB 608 (CA) 615 (Denning LJ).

[9] Nigel Tomkins, 'Getting Contributory Negligence Right' [2008] Journal of Personal Injury Law 196, 197.

and potential litigants and their advisers can be reasonably confident of the extent to which damages will be reduced for contributory negligence if the case reaches court, and this should help them to settle their dispute.

(3) Scope and Structure

Jurisdictions. This book is concerned with the law of contributory negligence in all parts of the United Kingdom. The relevant law is substantially uniform across the country.[10] **1.05**

Litigation vs settlements. The material on which reliance is placed in this book (including the empirical data) has been gathered from judicial decisions. No attempt has been made to investigate the operation of the law of contributory negligence in the settlement process, partly because several such studies already exist,[11] and partly because it is very challenging to obtain accurate and representative information regarding settlements. **1.06**

Structure of the book. In Part II we set out the principles and rules that comprise the contributory negligence doctrine and make some general observations about the way the doctrine operates in practice. In Part III we consider a series of frequently recurring fact situations in which the courts have imposed discounts for contributory negligence, focusing on the apportionment exercise. **1.07**

Contributory Negligence in the Twenty-First Century. As will be apparent from the length of this book, it prioritizes brevity and simplicity. Readers who are interested in a more comprehensive empirical exposition of the way in which the law of contributory negligence is applied by the courts, that emphasizes context over the black-letter law, are referred to this volume's companion work, *Contributory Negligence in the Twenty-First Century*.[12] **1.08**

---

[10] 'As one would expect, given that section 1(1) [of the Law Reform (Contributory Negligence) Act 1945] applies throughout the United Kingdom, the same approach has been followed in Scotland': *Jackson v Murray* [2015] UKSC 5, [2015] 2 All ER 805 [32] (Lord Reed).

[11] Studies of the law of contributory negligence in the context of settlements are offered in *Report of the Royal Commission on Civil Liability and Compensation for Personal Injury* (Cmnd 7054, 1978) vol 2, 163 (Table 117); *Report of the National Committee of Inquiry on Compensation and Rehabilitation in Australia* (Australian Government Publishing Service 1974) vol 1, paras 129–130; Donald Harris et al, *Compensation and Support for Illness and Injury* (Clarendon Press 1984) 91, 111; Law Commission, *Personal Injury Compensation: How Much is Enough? A Study of the Compensation Experiences of Victims of Personal Injury Law* (Law Com No 225, 1994) 81–82.

[12] James Goudkamp and Donal Nolan, *Contributory Negligence in the Twenty-First Century* (OUP forthcoming).

Part II

2

THE CONTRIBUTORY NEGLIGENCE DOCTRINE

(1) The Scope of the Doctrine

Causes of action to which the doctrine applies. The main cause of action to which the contributory negligence doctrine is relevant is, of course, the action in negligence. It applies also to claims for breach of statutory duty.[1] Where the claimant sues both for breach of a contractual duty to take reasonable care and in the tort of negligence, the doctrine will apply to both actions (unless the parties have excluded it by their agreement),[2] and in such a case the claimant cannot avoid the doctrine's application by suing only for breach of contract. Claims under section 2(1) of the Misrepresentation Act 1967 are similarly subject to the contributory negligence doctrine where liability also arises concurrently in the tort of negligence.[3] Claims based on the Consumer Protection Act 1987 are subject to the law of contributory negligence,[4] as are, it seems, claims in public nuisance,[5] as well as dependency claims in respect of fatal accidents.[6] **2.01**

Causes of action to which the doctrine does not apply. The contributory negligence doctrine does not apply to proceedings in deceit,[7] inducing a breach of contract,[8] or conspiracy.[9] Nor does it extend to claims in trespass to the person,[10] **2.02**

---

1 *Caswell v Powell Duffryn Associated Collieries Ltd* [1940] AC 152 (HL).

2 *Forsikringsaktieselskapet Vesta v Butcher* [1989] AC 852 (CA).

3 *Gran Gelato Ltd v Richcliff (Group) Ltd* [1992] Ch 560 (Ch D).

4 Consumer Protection Act 1987, s 6(4).

5 *Caswell v Powell Duffryn Associated Collieries Ltd* [1940] AC 152 (HL) 165 (Lord Atkin); *Trevett v Lee* [1955] 1 WLR 113 (CA) 122 (Evershed MR).

6 Fatal Accidents Act 1976, s 5.

7 *Standard Chartered Bank v Pakistan National Shipping Corp (Nos 2 and 4)* [2003] UKHL 43, [2003] 1 AC 959 [10]–[18] (Lord Hoffmann), [42]–[45] (Lord Rodger).

8 *Corporacion Nacional del Cobre de Chile v Sogemin Metals Ltd* [1997] 1 WLR 1396 (Ch D) 1405 (Carnwath J).

9 ibid; *Dellabarca v Northern Storemen and Packers Union* [1989] 2 NZLR 734 (HC) 757 (Smellie J).

10 *Horkin v North Melbourne Football Club Social Club* [1983] 1 VR 153 (SC) (battery); *Pritchard v Co-operative Group Ltd* [2011] EWCA Civ 329, [2012] QB 320 (battery); *McAleer v*

conversion, or trespass to goods.[11] The doctrine is also inapplicable to claims based on an asserted breach of a strict contractual duty,[12] and to claims where there is a contractual duty to take reasonable care where no concurrent duty is owed in the tort of negligence, although such cases can be expected to be relatively rare[13] following the acceptance of concurrent liability in tort and contract by the House of Lords in *Henderson v Merrett Syndicates (No 1)*.[14] It seems likely that where a claim is brought under section 2(1) of the Misrepresentation Act 1967 but no concurrent claim lies in the tort of negligence, the former claim cannot be met by the plea of contributory negligence.[15] The law of contributory negligence does not apply to actions for breach of confidence.[16]

2.03 **Causes of action where it is uncertain whether the doctrine applies.** It is unclear whether the contributory negligence doctrine extends to actions for breach of fiduciary duty. The High Court of Australia[17] held that it does not. The courts in New Zealand have not reached a definite position on the issue.[18] In Scots law, it has been held that the doctrine applies at least where the breach of fiduciary duty is unintentional.[19] The English authorities oppose the doctrine's application[20] and do likewise in relation to the action for breach of trust.[21] It is unclear whether the doctrine extends to the action on the case for injury to a reversionary interest, which is an action that persons with certain types of proprietary interests in property can invoke in respect of damage to the property concerned where they cannot sue in conversion or trespass because they were out of possession and did not have a right immediately to possess the property when it was damaged. Andrew Tettenborn suggests that such actions are subject to the law

---

Chief Constable of the PSNI [2014] NIQB 53 (battery); *Hicks v Young* [2015] EWHC 1144 (QB) (false imprisonment).

[11] Section 11(1) of the Torts (Interference with Goods) Act 1977 provides: 'Contributory negligence is no defence in proceedings founded on conversion, or on intentional trespass to goods.' Despite s 11(1), the contributory negligence doctrine applies in certain conversion claims in respect of cheques: Banking Act 1979, s 47 ('In any circumstances in which proof of absence of negligence on the part of a banker would be a defence in proceedings by reason of section 4 of the Cheques Act 1957, a defence of contributory negligence shall also be available to the banker notwithstanding the provisions of section 11(1) of the Torts (Interference with Goods) Act 1977').

[12] *Forsikringsaktieselskapet Vesta v Butcher* [1989] AC 852 (CA).

[13] Although see *Raflatac Ltd v Eade* [1999] 1 Lloyd's Rep 506 (QBD).

[14] [1995] 2 AC 145 (HL).

[15] Consider *Gran Gelato Ltd v Richcliff (Group) Ltd* [1992] Ch 560 (CA) 574 (Sir Donald Nicholls V-C).

[16] *Mosley v News Group Newspapers Ltd* [2008] EWHC 1777 (QB), [2008] EMLR 20 [224] (Eady J).

[17] *Pilmer v Duke Group Ltd* [2001] HCA 31, (2001) 207 CLR 165.

[18] See *Day v Mead* [1987] 2 NZLR 443 (CA) 451–53 (Cooke P), 461–62 (Somers J), 468 (Casey J), 469 (Hillyer J); *Maruha Corp v Amaltal International Ltd* [2007] NZSC 40 [23] (Blanchard J).

[19] *Kidd v Paull & Williamsons LLP* [2017] CSOH 16 [69] (Lord Tyre).

[20] *Nationwide Building Society v Balmer Radmore* [1999] Lloyd's Rep PN 241 (Ch D) 281–82 (Blackburne J); *de Beer v Kanaar & Co (a firm)* [2002] EWHC 688 (Ch) [92] (Patten J).

[21] *de Beer v Kanaar & Co (a firm)* [2002] EWHC 688 (Ch) [92] (Patten J).

of contributory negligence,[22] although it seems that there is no authority that is directly relevant in this regard.

The rules regarding the doctrine's scope lack a clear rationale. There seems to be very little, if anything, to explain why the contributory negligence doctrine applies to certain causes of action but not to others. The law that has just been described appears to be the product of historical accident rather than the result of any logical development. It is not at all obvious, for example, why a claim for breach of a contractual duty to take reasonable care should be subject to the contributory negligence doctrine where there is a concurrent claim in the tort of negligence but not otherwise. Serious doubt exists as to whether the law here is satisfactory, since it means that a claimant owed two duties may be worse off than a claimant owed one. It is noteworthy that the High Court of Australia decided that the doctrine of contributory negligence is not applicable at all in claims for breach of contract.[23] Reservations can also be expressed regarding the applicability of the contributory negligence doctrine to claims under section 2(1) of the Misrepresentation Act 1967, since that section appears to treat persons who are liable under it as being liable as if the misrepresentation had 'been made fraudulently' and the contributory negligence doctrine does not apply to proceedings in deceit. **2.04**

It may be suggested that the relevant law can be accounted for on the ground that the contributory negligence doctrine does not apply where the defendant acted intentionally. However, this does not provide an adequate explanation. Consider, in this regard, the tort of conversion, to which the contributory negligence doctrine does not apply. That tort can be committed both innocently (as where a defendant buys at an auction property which, unbeknownst to him or her, belongs to someone other than the vendor) and dishonestly (as where a defendant deliberately destroys property he or she knows belongs to the claimant). It may be suggested, alternatively, that the current law regarding the availability of the contributory negligence doctrine can be explained on the basis that the doctrine does not apply to the so-called 'property' torts. Andrew Tettenborn, for example, speaks of 'English lawyers' dislike of apportionment solutions in English property law'[24] and observes that the inapplicability of the defence in such cases dovetails with the fact that, in the law of negligence, an owner does not owe third parties a duty of care to safeguard his or her own property. However, this understanding would not explain the existing law either: most of the torts to which the doctrine does not apply have no necessary connection with any property. And even if the current rules could be explained in this way, it is far from clear that there is a **2.05**

---

[22] Andrew Tettenborn, 'Damages in Conversion—The Exception or the Anomaly?' (1993) 52 CLJ 128, 144; Andrew Tettenborn, 'Reversionary Damage to Chattels' (1994) 53 CLJ 326, 340–41.

[23] *Astley v Austrust Ltd* [1999] HCA 6, (1999) 197 CLR 1. However, the effect of *Astley* was swiftly overturned by all Australian legislatures (see, eg, the Law Reform (Miscellaneous Provisions) Amendment Act (NSW) 2000, amending the Law Reform (Miscellaneous Provisions) Act (NSW) 1965).

[24] Tettenborn (1993) (n 22) 138.

compelling reason for singling out property torts for separate treatment as far as the law of contributory negligence is concerned.

2.06 The fact of the matter is that the entire law of contributory negligence gets off to a bad start because the rules regarding the doctrine's applicability lack any obvious justification. It is wholly unsatisfactory that the law in this area seems to have sprung up by historical accident and has not been developed by reference to any sound argument. The question of which causes of action should be subject to the contributory negligence doctrine has never been considered in any thoroughgoing way. Ultimately, the extent of the doctrine's application should be resolved by reference to the reason why the law recognizes a rule of contributory negligence in the first place, but unfortunately that, too, is a matter in respect of which there is little learning.

(2) The Existence of Contributory Negligence

2.07 **The elements of the doctrine.** C will be guilty of contributory negligence where: (i) C took less care for his or her own safety or interests than the reasonable person in C's position would have taken; and (ii) that failure was causally related to C's damage.[25]

(a) A failure by the claimant to take reasonable care of him or herself

2.08 **The claimant is required to take reasonable care.** It is often said, rightly or wrongly, that the same principles that determine whether a defendant failed to take reasonable care of the claimant's interests also control the circumstances in which a claimant will, for the purposes of the law of contributory negligence, be taken to have fallen short of the standard of care expected of him or her.[26] Hence, the claimant 'is not required to attain a standard of perfection'.[27] Rather, the standard that a claimant is expected to achieve is one of reasonable care only, which standard must take account of 'the realities of ordinary everyday life'.[28]

2.09 If the principles that govern the negligence enquiry apply also to the question whether the claimant took sufficient care of his or her own interests, it follows that it is relevant to consider matters such as the cost of taking precautions against the risk, the probability that the risk would materialize, the gravity of the harm

[25] *Nance v British Columbia Electric Railway Co Ltd* [1951] AC 601 (PC) 611 (Viscount Simon).

[26] See, eg, *Casson v Spotmix Ltd (in liq)* [2017] EWCA Civ 1994 [6] (Sir Terence Etherton MR) ('[I]t is uncontroversial that the standard of care [that the claimant must achieve] is the same as that applied when considering negligence from the perspective of breach of duty'). For discussion, see Kenneth Simons, 'Victim Fault and Victim Strict Responsibility in Anglo-American Tort Law' (2015) 8 Journal of Tort Law 29; Joachim Dietrich and Iain Field, 'The "Reasonable Tort Victim": Contributory Negligence, Standard of Care and the "Equivalence Theory"' (2017) 41 Melbourne University Law Review 602.

[27] *Crew v Ash* [2008] EWHC 3068 (QB) [28] (Lloyd Jones J).

[28] *Howe v Houlton* [2009] EWHC 3344 (QB) [123] (Swift J).

if the risk came to pass, and the utility of the claimant's conduct.[29] It also follows that the risk of harm that materialized must have been reasonably foreseeable by the claimant for a finding of contributory negligence to be made. As Denning LJ said in *Jones v Livox Quarries Ltd*, '[j]ust as actionable negligence requires the foreseeability of harm to others, so contributory negligence requires the foreseeability of harm to oneself'.[30] However, and again consistently with the rules by which it is determined whether the defendant was negligent, it is unnecessary that the claimant foresee 'the precise way that the damage or injury is caused'.[31]

Consistently with the fact that claimants need take no more than reasonable care of themselves, claimants have been acquitted of contributory negligence in omitting to notice obstructions on the ground that there was no reason to expect would be present,[32] in failing to consult a doctor as soon as symptoms of a disease started to emerge,[33] on account of 'mere momentary inadvertence',[34] in slipping on a floor that the claimant had no reason to think would be wet,[35] in failing to ask a driver whether he was so impaired by alcohol consumption that he should not drive,[36] in not foreseeing the possibility that another driver would allow his vehicle to drift onto the claimant's side of the road[37] or that a car door would be opened unexpectedly,[38] in failing to evacuate a vehicle that had broken down[39] or been involved in an accident[40] and move to a safer position, and in not foreseeing that a lorry in a stream of traffic might pass too close to an open car door.[41] **2.10**

The reasonableness of the claimant's conduct is to be assessed at the time of the alleged contributory negligence. In asking whether the defendant failed to take reasonable care the court must ask how the reasonable person would have behaved at the time of the alleged negligence.[42] The defendant is not to be penalized because the standard of care of the reasonable person has increased by the time of the trial. The same rule has been adopted in the contributory negligence context.[43] **2.11**

29 *Gilfillan v Barbour* 2003 SLT 1127 (OH) is a good illustration of a case in which the utility of the claimant's conduct was relevant. See especially at 1135 (Lord Reed).

30 [1952] 2 QB 608 (CA) 615.

31 *Badger v Ministry of Defence* [2005] EWHC 2941 (QB), [2006] 3 All ER 173 [12] (Burnton J).

32 *Nimmo v Secretary of State for Scotland* 2000 Rep LR 14 (OH).

33 *Allen v British Rail Engineering Ltd* 1998 WL 1751101 (QBD).

34 *Casson v Spotmix Ltd (in liq)* [2017] EWCA Civ 1994 [7] (Sir Terence Etherton MR); *MacLachlan v Strathclyde Partnership for Transport* 2017 GWD 14-227 (Sheriff Personal Injury Court) [102] (Sheriff Fiona Lennox Reith QC).

35 *McLeish v Lothian NHS Board* [2017] CSOH 71, 2017 Rep LR 90 [8] (Lord Mulholland).

36 *Booth v White* [2003] EWCA Civ 1708.

37 *Gray v Gibson* [2014] EWCA Civ 355.

38 *Burridge v Air Work Ltd* [2004] EWCA Civ 459.

39 *Hughes v Guise Motors Ltd* [2007] EWHC 2529 (QB).

40 *Lac v Clayton* [2009] EWCA Civ 106.

41 *Howe v Houlton* [2009] EWHC 3344 (QB).

42 *Roe v Ministry of Health* [1954] 2 QB 66 (CA).

43 See, eg, *Smith v Finch* [2009] EWHC 53 (QB) [43] (Griffith Williams J).

2.12 **Reasonable care may require anticipating carelessness by others.** The taking of reasonable care may require the claimant to anticipate that others will be careless and to take appropriate precautions against that risk. As Denning LJ said, '[a] person is guilty of contributory negligence if he ought reasonably to have foreseen that, if he did not act as a reasonable, prudent man, he might be hurt himself; and in his reckonings he must take into account the possibility of others being careless'.[44] A good illustration of this rule is the passenger who accepts a lift from a driver he or she knows is intoxicated. Exceptional cases aside, such as where the only alternative to accepting a lift would be having to walk an unknown distance over unfamiliar territory at night-time,[45] such a passenger is very likely to be found guilty of contributory negligence.[46] *McDermott v Pettit*[47] is another example of the same principle. In that case, Parker J, in holding the claimant pedestrian guilty of contributory negligence, remarked that the claimant should have anticipated the possibility that some motorists would be intoxicated at 2.30 am.[48] And in a claim by a government department against a law firm, the judge held that the department was guilty of contributory negligence because it should have had its own system in place for ensuring that it made a vital payment that would have enabled it to exercise a break clause in a lease on time, and ought not to have relied completely on its legal advisers to remind it of the need to make the payment.[49]

2.13 However, in certain circumstances, a claimant may be justified in assuming that others will take reasonable care and hence not taking precautions to guard against the risk of their negligence. For example, in *Gray v Gibson*[50] it was found that a reasonable motorist in the claimant's position would not have foreseen the risk that the driver of a lorry would move onto the claimant's side of the road when rounding a bend. Similarly, in *Whyte v Bluebird Buses Ltd*, where the pursuer was injured by a bus that intruded onto the pavement, the judge rejected the plea of contributory negligence, remarking that '[t]he pursuer, wholly on the pavement, is entitled not to be struck by a vehicle'.[51] An important context in which a claimant will generally be entitled to assume that another will take reasonable care of the claimant's interests is that of professional negligence. That setting is considered later.[52]

---

44 *Jones v Livox Quarries Ltd* [1952] 2 QB 608 (CA) 615.

45 See, eg, *Allen v Chadwick* [2015] HCA 47, (2015) 256 CLR 148 [61] (French CJ, Kiefel, Bell, Keane and Gordon JJ).

46 In *Owens v Brimmell* [1977] QB 859 (QBD) 866, Watkins J said that 'there is widespread and weighty authority for the proposition that a passenger may be guilty of contributory negligence if he rides with the driver of a car whom he knows has consumed alcohol in such quantity as is likely to impair to a dangerous degree that driver's capacity to drive properly and safely'.

47 [2011] EWHC 3074 (QB).

48 ibid [31].

49 *Secretary of State for the Environment, Transport and the Regions v Unicorn Consultancy Services Ltd* [2000] NPC 108 (Ch D). For similar reasoning in a Canadian case, see *Doiron v Caisse Populaire* (1985) 17 DLR (4th) 660 (NBCA), where the court held that a financial institution was guilty of contributory negligence for failing to check that the loan documents provided by the defendant solicitor complied with its instructions.

50 [2014] EWCA Civ 355 [20] (Longmore LJ).

51 [2015] CSOH 56 [28] (Lord McEwan). To like effect, see also *Osei-Antwi v South East London & Kent Bus Co Ltd* [2010] EWCA Civ 132 [17] (Hallett LJ).

52 See 2.26.

The fault must be self-regarding. Whereas the negligence that grounds liability consists in a failure to take reasonable care for the safety or interests of others, contributory negligence involves a failure by the claimant to take care of his or her own safety or interests.[53] Accordingly, the mere fact that a claimant failed to look out for the interests of others will not amount to contributory negligence. Consistently with that principle, the contributory negligence doctrine can be triggered despite the fact that the claimant did not owe the defendant (or anyone else) a relevant duty of care.[54] Nor is it necessary in order for the contributory negligence doctrine to apply that the claimant's fault be actionable at the instance of the defendant or a third party. Arguably, however, where the claimant did in fact owe the defendant or a third party a duty of care and the contributory negligence also amounted to a breach of that duty, that circumstance is (or should be) taken into account when apportioning responsibility for the claimant's damage. 2.14

An objective test. The standard of care that the claimant has to achieve is objective. Consequently, and as Lord Denning MR explained in *Froom v Butcher*, '[i]n determining [the issue of contributory negligence], the law eliminates the personal equation. It takes no notice of the views of the particular individual or of others like him. It requires everyone to exercise all such precautions as a man of ordinary prudence would observe.'[55] In other words, a claimant's idiosyncrasies should, in principle, be disregarded in determining whether he or she is guilty of contributory negligence. Thus, in *Froom* itself, it was irrelevant that the claimant believed, wrongly, that using a seat belt increases the chances of suffering serious injury. The adoption of an objective test also means that the fact that the claimant was incapable of achieving the standard of the reasonable person is irrelevant. The question 'is not whether the claimant's conduct fell below the standard reasonably to be expected of him, but whether it fell below the standard reasonably to be expected of a person in his position: did his conduct fall below the standard to be expected of a person of ordinary prudence?'.[56] 2.15

The main exception to the objective test: childhood. The most prominent exception to the objective test for contributory negligence is childhood, an exception that can be justified on the basis that childhood is not an idiosyncrasy.[57] 2.16

[53] *Froom v Butcher* [1976] QB 286 (CA) 291 (Lord Denning MR).

[54] See *Jones v Livox Quarries Ltd* [1952] 2 QB 608 (CA) 615 (Denning LJ): 'contributory negligence does not depend on [the existence of] a duty of care'. See also *Davies v Swan Motor Co (Swansea) Ltd* [1949] 2 KB 291 (CA) 324 (Denning LJ).

[55] [1976] QB 286 (CA) 294.

[56] *Badger v Ministry of Defence* [2005] EWHC 2941 (QB), [2006] 3 All ER 173 [7] (Stanley Burnton J).

[57] Consider the remarks in *McHale v Watson* (1966) 115 CLR 199 (HCA) 213 (Kitto J) ('The standard of care being objective, it is no answer for him, any more than it is for an adult, to say that the harm he caused was due to his being abnormally slow-witted, quick-tempered, absent-minded or inexperienced. But it does not follow that he cannot rely in his defence upon a limitation upon the capacity for foresight or prudence, not as being personal to himself, but as being characteristic of humanity at his stage of development and in that sense normal. By doing so he appeals to a standard of ordinariness, to an objective and not a subjective standard').

Where the claimant is a child, the claimant's conduct will be judged against the benchmark of the reasonable child of the same age.[58] The reasonable child is neither 'a paragon of prudence' nor 'a scatter-brained child' but the 'ordinary child'.[59] Although there is no fixed age below which the courts regard findings of contributory negligence as impermissible, it seems that where the claimant is so young that he or she is incapable of taking any care, there is no scope for holding the claimant guilty of contributory negligence. In *Gardner v Grace*, Channell B declared that '[t]he doctrine of contributory negligence does not apply to an infant of tender age',[60] and in *Gough v Thorne* Lord Denning MR remarked:[61]

> A very young child cannot be guilty of contributory negligence. An older child may be. But it depends on the circumstances. A judge should only find a child guilty of contributory negligence if he or she is of such an age as to be expected to take precautions for his or her own safety: and then he or she is only to be found guilty if blame should be attached to him or her. A child has not the road sense or the experience of his or her elders. He or she is not to be found guilty unless he or she is blameworthy.

2.17 In *Re Kelly v Nugent*,[62] Gillen J suggested that it will be a borderline issue as to whether a child aged nine is capable of taking any care, although a child aged seven was found guilty of contributory negligence in a recent English case,[63] and there are older Scottish decisions (which would, however, possibly be decided differently today) in which the doctrine of contributory negligence was applied to children aged as young as four.[64] In *Boardman v Ministry of Defence*,[65] the judge considered that no blame could attach to a six-year-old boy who had run into the road regardless of the reason why he entered the carriageway, but in *AB v Main*, HHJ Davies considered that an ordinary child aged nine would 'know of the importance of looking right and left to check for oncoming traffic before crossing'[66] a road. Where the defendant's negligence created a dangerous situation that acted as an 'allurement' to children, the court may be disinclined to find contributory negligence.[67] In contrast with the position that prevails in relation to childhood, the courts do not seem disposed to make any allowances for the claimant's reduced ability to look after themselves on account of their advanced age.[68]

---

[58] See, eg, *C v Imperial Design Ltd* [2001] Env LR 33 (CA) [39] (Arden LJ).

[59] *Gough v Thorne* [1966] 1 WLR 1387 (CA) 1391 (Salmon LJ).

[60] (1858) 1 F & F 359, 359; 175 ER 763, 763.

[61] [1966] 1 WLR 1387 (CA) 1390.

[62] [2011] NIQB 79 [21].

[63] *N (a child) v Newham LBC* [2007] CLY 2931 (Central London CC) (the claimant punched a pane of glass while at school).

[64] *Cass v Edinburgh & District Tramways Co Ltd* 1909 SC 1068 (IH) (four); *McKinnell v White* 1971 SLT 61 (notes) (OH) (five); *Banner's Tutor v Kennedy's Trustees* 1978 SLT (notes) (OH) 85 (five); *Harvey v Cairns* 1989 SLT 107 (OH) (six).

[65] QBD, 12 November 2012 [24] (HHJ Hawkesworth QC).

[66] [2015] EWHC 3183 (QB) [95].

[67] *Galbraith's Curator ad Litem v Stewart (No 2)* 1998 SLT 1305 (OH).

[68] Consider, eg, *Maughan v Boylan* [2006] NIQB 38; *Moreh v O'Neill* [2008] NIQB 28.

Despite the fact that the existence of the childhood exception to the objective standard operates in favour of child claimants, empirical evidence suggests that such claimants are nevertheless more likely to be found guilty of contributory negligence than adults. According to the relevant study of first instance claims, the plea of contributory negligence succeeded in 62% of the claims where the claimant was known to be an adult, and in 72% of claims where the claimant was known to be a child.[69] Of course, this result may be explicable in large part on the ground that younger claimants tend to act more irresponsibly. However, the figure is nonetheless striking and gives rise to some doubt as to the accuracy of the common perception[70] that the courts treat child claimants leniently with regard to contributory negligence. 2.18

Other exceptions to the objective test. Other exceptions to the objective test for contributory negligence have been recognized on a more ad hoc and sporadic basis and generally without any attempt to explain their recognition. In *Spearman v United Bath Hospitals NHS Foundation Trust*, Spencer J refused to hold that a mentally ill person, who suffered injury following his either falling or jumping off a roof, was guilty of contributory negligence. The judge said:[71] 2.19

> Just as a young child is not guilty of contributory negligence in running out into a road where the child is so young as not to appreciate the danger of so doing, so too where a person's state of mind is such that, whether temporarily or permanently, they do not appreciate that they are putting themselves in danger and it cannot be said that they should have so appreciated. Otherwise, that would be to penalise a person for being ill or of unsound mind, and the law does not do that.

In effect, Spencer J imputed the claimant's mental illness to the reasonable person with the result that the claimant did not take less care than the reasonable person in his position would have taken.[72] In *Allen v British Rail Engineering Ltd*, Smith J, in rejecting the suggestion that a claimant was guilty of contributory negligence in failing to consult a doctor regarding symptoms from which he was suffering, took account of the claimant's stoicism.[73] In *Lac v Clayton*,[74] regard was had to the fact that the claimants had been shaken on account of their having been involved in a collision in deciding whether they took reasonable care of their own safety thereafter. And in a claim against a law firm the judge took account, in finding that there was no contributory negligence, of the fact that the person who ran

[69] James Goudkamp and Donal Nolan, 'Contributory Negligence in the Twenty-First Century: An Empirical Study of First Instance Decisions' (2016) 79 MLR 575, 602. For fuller discussion of this and other results relating to age in the study, see ibid 608–10.

[70] See, eg, Caroline Sappideen and Prue Vines (eds), *Fleming's The Law of Torts* (10th edn, Thomson Reuters Professional (Australia) Ltd 2011) 330 ('The courts have been singularly lenient to children ... in terms of finding them guilty of contributory negligence').

[71] [2017] EWHC 3027 (QB) [74].

[72] Conversely, in proceedings in negligence, no allowance is made for mental illness suffered by the defendant, however severe: *Dunnage v Randall* [2015] EWCA Civ 673, [2016] QB 639.

[73] 1998 WL 1751101 (QBD) [123].

[74] [2009] EWCA Civ 106 [20]–[21] (Smith LJ).

the claimant company had 'little or no experience' of property development and limited understanding of the 'intricacies of [such] agreements'.[75]

2.20 **Claimant engaged in a repetitive activity on the defendant's behalf.** Ordinarily, both in the law of negligence and the law of contributory negligence, the specific conduct of the defendant or claimant that led to the damage is the focus of the court's attention. The question is whether that precise conduct fell below the standard of the reasonable person. The fact that the actor may have behaved competently in the hours, weeks, and months previously is generally irrelevant when it comes to deciding whether the actor behaved reasonably on the occasion in question. For example, it is no answer for a driver who made a negligent error to say that he or she usually drove well.[76] The law of contributory negligence recognizes an exception to this principle. Where the claimant was required by the defendant to engage in a repetitive activity and, in the course of that activity, made an error that resulted in his or her suffering damage, that error will not be judged in isolation for the purposes of determining whether it constitutes contributory negligence. Rather, account will be taken of the repetitive nature of the work that the claimant was required to do and the fatigue and tedium that it was likely to induce. In such a case, provided that the claimant generally acted carefully, the court will be unlikely to make a finding of contributory negligence.[77] An alternative way of understanding the law of contributory negligence in the context of repetitive activities is not as an exception to the principle that generally acting reasonably is no answer to an allegation of carelessness but as qualifying the objective standard of care. On this way of looking at things, the fatigue and tedium experienced by the claimant borne of the repetitive nature of his or her activity will be imputed to the reasonable person for the purposes of ascertaining whether the claimant took reasonable care in the circumstances.

2.21 The principle that allowances should be made for claimants who are engaged in a repetitive activity on behalf of the defendant applies, classically, in the context of manual labour. In *Flower v Ebbw Vale Steel Iron & Coal Ltd*, Lord Wright quoted with approval the trial judge's remark that 'it is not for every risky thing which a workman in a factory may do in his familiarity with the machinery that a plaintiff ought to be held guilty of contributory negligence'.[78]

2.22 **Defendant under a duty to prevent carelessness by the claimant.** The understanding discussed in the previous paragraph applies a fortiori where the defendant was obliged by legislation or regulation to take precautions to prevent

75 *Akasuc Enterprise Ltd v Farmar & Shirreff (a firm)* [2003] EWHC 1275 (Ch) [21], [80] (Peter Smith J).

76 cf s 3 of the Social Action, Responsibility and Heroism Act 2015, which provides: 'the court must have regard to whether the person, in carrying out the activity in the course of which the alleged negligence or breach of statutory duty occurred, demonstrated a predominantly responsible approach towards protecting the safety or other interests of others'. Regarding this provision, see James Goudkamp, 'Restating the Common Law? The Social Action, Responsibility and Heroism Act 2015' (2017) 37 Legal Studies 577, 591–93.

77 *Caswell v Powell Duffryn Associated Collieries Ltd* [1940] AC 152 (HL) 187 (Lord Porter).

78 [1936] AC 206 (HL) 214.

carelessness of the kind in question. In such circumstances, the claimant's carelessness will tend merely to establish that the defendant failed to comply with his or her duty. As Goddard LJ said in *Hutchinson v London & North Eastern Railway Co*:[79]

> It is only too common to find in cases where the plaintiff alleges that a defendant employer has been guilty of breach of a statutory duty, that a plea of contributory negligence has been set up. In such a case I always directed myself to be exceedingly chary of finding contributory negligence where the contributory negligence alleged was the very thing which the statutory duty of the employer was designed to prevent.

Although these remarks were made prior to the introduction of the apportionment legislation, the courts have remained faithful to the principle,[80] which appears to be at least partially rooted in the idea that findings of contributory negligence in such cases might undermine the objectives of the legislation imposing the duty on the defendant. By parity of reasoning, the courts ought to be wary of finding contributory negligence where the defendant owed a common law duty that obliged him or her to prevent the very conduct that is said to amount to contributory negligence, although authority that is directly on point is harder to find.

Claimant confronted with an emergency. The claimant will usually be forgiven if he or she has made the wrong choice, or acted less than ideally, when confronted with an emergency created by the defendant, or was otherwise placed under considerable pressure by the defendant. For example, in *Rickson v Bhakar,* Blake J said: 'a person placed in a situation of responding to a danger created by another cannot be considered guilty of negligence merely because one of two available options turns out to be less effective'.[81] However, claimants will sometimes be expected to act quickly when faced with a need for instant action,[82] and a claimant may be guilty of contributory negligence if they were responsible for the predicament in which they found themselves.[83] **2.23**

Relevance of the fact that other persons acted similarly. In determining whether the claimant took reasonable care for their own safety or interests, it may be **2.24**

[79] [1942] 1 KB 481 (CA) 488.

[80] See, eg, *Staveley Iron & Chemical Co Ltd v Jones* [1956] AC 627 (HL) 648 (Lord Tucker) ('in Factory Act cases the purpose of imposing the absolute obligation is to protect the workmen against those very acts of inattention which are sometimes relied upon as constituting contributory negligence so that too strict a standard would defeat the object of the statute'). See also *Ashbridge v Christian Salvensen Plc* [2006] CSOH 79 2006 SLT 697 [25] (Lord Glennie).

[81] [2017] EWHC 264 (QB) [31]. See also *Crew v Ash* [2008] EWHC 3068 (QB) [23] (Lloyd Jones J); *Dickson v Kinsman* [2013] CSOH 111[47]–[48] (Lord Boyd); *Nadarajah v Sotnick* [2013] EWHC 3389 (QB) [47] (Carr J).

[82] See, eg, *Malcolm v Commissioner of Police of the Metropolis* 1999 WL 477408 (QBD) (claimant guilty of contributory negligence in failing to remove arm from lift doors after it became apparent that they would not be automatically retracted); *Bennett v Southwell* [2013] EWHC 2382 (QB) (claimant guilty of contributory negligence in becoming distracted and in steering into the path of an oncoming vehicle despite being startled by its sudden presence on her side of the road).

[83] See, eg, *Hickman v London Central Bus Co Ltd* [2013] EWHC 1703 (QB) [64]–[66] (Sir Robert Nelson).

relevant to ask whether other persons situated in the same position as the claimant behaved in a like manner. If the claimant acted in much the same way as similarly situated persons, that will tend to suggest that what the claimant did was not unreasonable. In *Casson v Spotmix Ltd (in liq)*, the claimant employee suffered injury to his hand while cleaning a machine. Sir Terence Etherton MR said:[84]

> [T]he fact that every other employee charged with the task of cleaning the machine did exactly what the claimant did is strongly supportive of the conclusion that the extent to which the claimant's conduct could be criticised fell considerably short of that which could properly be categorised as amounting to contributory negligence.

2.25 *Webb Resolutions Ltd v E.Surv Ltd*[85] involved a claim by a lender against surveyors. In considering whether the lender was guilty of contributory negligence, Coulson J said: 'In general terms, the approach is to see what was happening elsewhere in the lending market because, if the claimant was doing what its competitors were doing, negligence was unlikely, unless it could be shown that it was irrational or illogical.'[86]

2.26 **The professional negligence context.** The courts seem to treat professional negligence cases differently from other types of case as far as contributory negligence is concerned. According to a recent empirical study of the operation of the contributory negligence doctrine in courts of first instance, the average success rate of the plea of contributory negligence was much lower in professional negligence claims (29%) than in all the claims sampled (60%).[87] There are obvious reasons why a professional will often face 'grave difficulty'[88] and will 'only rarely … be able to set up allegations of contributory negligence against their clients'.[89] These reasons include the fact that the professional will usually have greater expertise than the client in the relevant field, that the relationship between professional and client is often markedly asymmetrical in terms of power, and that it will often be reasonable for the client to follow professional advice and to rely on the professional to do properly the job that he or she has been engaged to do. It appears that the courts are particularly reluctant to find that claimants are guilty of

---

84 [2017] EWCA Civ 1994 [15].

85 [2012] EWHC 3653 (TCC), [2013] PNLR 15.

86 ibid [71]. See also *Paratus AMC Ltd v Countrywide Surveyors Ltd* [2011] EWHC 3307 (Ch), [2012] PNLR 12 [79]–[80] (HHJ Keyser); *Barclays Bank Plc v Christie Owen & Davies Ltd* [2016] EWHC 2351 (Ch), [2017] PNLR 8 [232] (Richard Spearman QC) ('if a practice was accepted by a significant section of the banking market at the relevant time, it should not be held to fail to meet the standard of a reasonably competent bank unless plainly illogical').

87 Goudkamp and Nolan (n 69) 592. See, further, James Goudkamp and Donal Nolan, 'Contributory Negligence and Professional Negligence: An Empirical Perspective' in Kit Barker and Ross Grantham (eds), *Apportionment in Private Law* (Hart 2019) (forthcoming).

88 David Marks, 'Professional Negligence: Contribution and Contributory Negligence' (1988–1989) 15 University of Queensland Law Journal 209, 226–27.

89 *Secretary of State for the Environment, Transport and the Regions v Unicorn Consultancy Services Ltd* [2000] NPC 108 (Ch D) [128] (Rimer J).

contributory negligence in the medical negligence context, with there being just a single reported case in England in which the plea of contributory negligence succeeded in that setting.[90]

It seems that contributory negligence will be especially hard to establish where the alleged carelessness comprises a failure by the claimant client to detect an error committed by the defendant professional or to remember to do something which it was the responsibility of the defendant to remind the claimant to do. In *Credit Lyonnais SA v Russell Jones & Walker (a firm)*,[91] for example, the defendant law firm had been negligent in not drawing to its client's attention the fact that time was of the essence in relation to a particular payment that needed to be made in order to exercise a break clause in a lease. The defendant's argument that the claimant (a major bank) had also been guilty of contributory negligence in not making the payment on time was rejected. Similarly, in *Akasuc Enterprise Ltd v Farmar & Shirreff (a firm)*,[92] where the defendant's negligence involved failing to insert a mechanism into a conditional purchase agreement to protect an overage fee, the judge rejected the argument that the corporate client in question had been negligent in not noticing the omission. And in *Feakins v Burstow*,[93] it was said that it would be rare for a client alleging the negligence of a lawyer in the conduct of litigation to be found guilty of contributory fault. Finally, in a case where insurance underwriters had settled a claim in reliance on defective advice provided by their solicitors, Simon J gave short shrift to the defendant's allegation that the claimants had been guilty of contributory negligence in not realizing that the advice it had given was flawed. The judge remarked that:[94] **2.27**

> The defendant was specifically instructed to consider the issue of coverage and it is difficult to see why the client, who has paid the solicitor to do the work, should check that the solicitor has done the task for which he has been employed ... To put the matter more proverbially: if you hire a dog you do not expect to have to bark.

---

[90] *Pidgeon v Doncaster HA* [2002] Lloyd's Rep Med 130 (Sheffield CC). For discussion, see Robert Harper, 'The Application of Contributory Negligence Principles to the Doctor/Patient Relationship' (2001) 9 Torts Law Journal 1; Yola Ventresca, Peter Kryworuk, and Scott Chambers, 'With Patient Rights Come Patient Responsibilities: Contributory Negligence in Medical Negligence Actions' (2007) 33 Advocates' Quarterly 207; Jonathan Herring and Charles Foster, 'Blaming the Patient: Contributory Negligence in Medical Malpractice Litigation' (2009) 25 Professional Negligence 76.

[91] [2002] EWHC 1310 (Ch), [2003] PNLR 2; cf *Secretary of State for the Environment, Transport and the Regions v Unicorn Consultancy Services Ltd* (2000) NPC 108 (Ch D).

[92] [2003] EWHC 1275 (Ch).

[93] [2005] EWHC 1931 (QB), [2006] PNLR 6.

[94] *Newline Corporate Name Ltd v Morgan Cole (a firm)* [2007] EWHC 1628 (Comm), [2008] PNLR 2 [69]. For the same argument in respect of other types of professional adviser, see *Chrysalis Scotland Ltd v Clydesdale Bank Insurance Brokers Ltd* [2008] CSOH 144 [58] (Lord Glennie) (financial adviser); *Manorgate Ltd v First Scottish Property Services Ltd* [2013] CSOH 108 [58] (Lord Woolman) (property search company).

2.28 Conversely, in professional negligence cases the courts are more willing to find contributory negligence where there was carelessness on the part of the claimant that was independent of the defendant's fault, such as occurs where an institutional lender loses money on account of having lent money due to both a negligent valuation and improper lending practices. Failures to comply with the standard of the reasonable lender have included not taking account of discrepancies between a borrower's statements as to his debts and those revealed by credit checks;[95] failing to make enquiries regarding a borrower's income and ability to service the loan;[96] failing to take account of a borrower's misuse of an earlier loan;[97] and lending sums of money for a project that the lender knew exceeded the project's cost.[98] Furthermore, in cases of this kind, a sophisticated lender may be held to have been at fault simply for not second-guessing the valuation provided by the defendant, though in such a scenario a lower discount can be expected.[99]

2.29 **Rescuers.** It has long been the clear policy of the law to encourage rescue.[100] Thus, the courts have been reluctant to hold rescuers who make matters worse liable in negligence,[101] and have been similarly slow, where the rescuer is injured, to hold that the rescuer was *volens* to the risk of injury.[102] Likewise, the courts are hesitant to conclude that it was contributorily negligent of an injured rescuer to intervene. As Lord Steyn said in *White v Chief Constable of South Yorkshire*:[103]

> The law has long recognised the moral imperative of encouraging citizens to rescue persons in peril. Those who altruistically expose themselves to danger in an emergency to save others are favoured by the law ... A plea of contributory negligence will usually receive short shrift.

---

95 See, eg, *Paratus AMC Ltd v Countrywide Surveyors Ltd* [2011] EWHC 3307 (Ch), [2012] PNLR 12; *Webb Resolutions Ltd v E.Surv Ltd* [2012] EWHC 3653 (TCC), [2013] PNLR 15.

96 See, eg, *Paratus AMC Ltd v Countrywide Surveyors Ltd* [2011] EWHC 3307 (Ch), [2012] PNLR 12.

97 See, eg, *Barclays Bank Plc v Christie Owen & Davies Ltd* [2016] EWHC 2351 (Ch), [2017] PNLR 8.

98 See, eg, *Lloyds Bank Plc v McBains Cooper Consulting Ltd* [2018] EWCA Civ 452.

99 See, eg, *Speshal Investments Ltd v Corby Kane Howard Partnership Ltd* [2003] EWHC 390 (Ch) (20% discount for failing to subject to critical analysis the disparity between the purchase price of the properties against which the loan was secured and the valuations provided by the defendants).

100 A dated but still the best analysis of how tort law applies in rescue situations is AM Linden 'Rescuers and Good Samaritans' (1972) 10 Alberta Law Review 89.

101 'The saving of life or limb justifies taking considerable risk': *Watt v Hertfordshire CC* [1954] 1 WLR 835 (CA) 838 (Denning LJ). See also at 838 (Singleton LJ) and the Social Action, Responsibility and Heroism Act 2015, s 4, which provides: 'The court must have regard to whether the alleged negligence or breach of statutory duty occurred when the person was acting heroically by intervening in an emergency to assist an individual in danger.' For discussion of this provision, see Goudkamp (n 76) 594–95.

102 *Haynes v Harwood* [1935] 1 KB 146 (CA); *Baker v TE Hopkins & Son Ltd* [1959] 1 WLR 966 (CA) 976 (Morris LJ), 979 (Omerod LJ), 983 (Wilmer LJ). As to the connection between the law of contributory negligence and the doctrine of voluntary assumption of risk, see 4.09–4.10.

103 [1999] 2 AC 455 (HL) 498.

Similarly, in *Tolley v Carr*, Hickinbottom J said that '[t]he law recognises that a rescuer may, in effecting or attempting to effect a reduction of risk to others, imperil of his own life and limb: and the greater the risk to others that he is trying to avert, the greater the imperilment to his safety the law will accept as reasonable'.[104] Hickinbottom J added that 'exceptional bravery is not the same as foolhardiness'.[105] Nonetheless, rescuers have occasionally been found guilty of contributory negligence. In *Sparrow v Andre*,[106] the claimant was injured when he attempted physically to stop a car containing his young children from rolling down a slope towards an electrical switch room and propane gas cylinders. The claimant had accidentally left the car with the ignition switched on and in 'neutral' instead of 'park' mode. The court held that contributory negligence was established, apparently partly on the basis of the claimant's conduct in endeavouring to arrest the movement of the vehicle. **2.30**

Criminal conduct. Criminal conduct will often amount to fault for the purposes of the law of contributory negligence. Speeding[107] is a good illustration of a violation of the criminal law that will almost always, when causally connected to the claimant's damage, constitute contributory negligence.[108] Another classic illustration of criminal conduct that is very likely to constitute contributory negligence if causally relevant is failure to wear a seat belt in a vehicle.[109] In *Froom v Butcher*, the Court of Appeal held that a person who 'fails to wear [a seat belt] must share some responsibility for the damage'.[110] **2.31**

Intentional self-harm. It might be thought that the notion that intentionally inflicted harm can constitute contributory negligence makes no sense on the basis that the idea of 'intentional negligence' is contradictory. However, this view involves a misunderstanding of the concept of negligence. Negligence, including contributory negligence, is a type of conduct, namely, behaviour that exhibits less care than the reasonable person would have taken in all of the circumstances. Accordingly, there is no reason why intentional conduct cannot amount to contributory negligence in an appropriate case. A conclusion to the contrary would in any event involve the peculiar outcome whereby a person who inadvertently **2.32**

[104] [2010] EWHC 2191 (QB), [2011] RTR 7 [22].

[105] ibid [47]. See also *Baker v TE Hopkins & Son Ltd* [1959] 1 WLR 966 (CA) 976–77 (Morris LJ), 979–80 (Ormerod LJ), 984–85 (Wilmer LJ).

[106] [2016] EWHC 739 (QB).

[107] Including by bicyclists: see *Daly v Heeps* 2018 GWD 2-45 (Lothian and Borders Sheriff Court) [35] (Sheriff Peter J Braid).

[108] See, eg, *Buchan v Whiting* [2008] EWHC 2951 (QB); *Train v Secretary of State for Defence* [2014] EWHC 1928 (QB); *Buswell v Symes* [2015] EWHC 1379 (QB). However, no negligence can be inferred simply from the fact that a person, such as a police officer, lawfully drove in excess of the designated speed limit: *Gilfillan v Barbour* 2003 SLT 1127 (OH) [31] (Lord Reed).

[109] Unless the claimant was exempt from the requirement to wear a seat belt: *Jones v Morgan* [1994] CLY 3344 (EWHC). For an exceptional case in which the claimants were held not guilty of contributory negligence in accepting a ride in the back of a van that was not fitted with seat belts because it had been designed to carry goods rather than people, see *Cross v Smith* 1999 WL 982463 (CA).

[110] [1976] QB 286 (CA) 295 (Lord Denning MR).

but carelessly caused themselves harm would be liable to have their damages reduced for contributory negligence, but a person who engaged in acts of deliberate self-harm would not. After a period of some confusion, the courts confirmed that a claimant's intentional self-harm can constitute contributory negligence. The leading case is *Reeves v Commissioner of the Police of the Metropolis*.[111] The deceased had committed suicide while in police custody. A claim by his dependants and on behalf of the deceased's estate succeeded on the basis that the police had been negligent in not taking precautions to prevent the deceased killing himself, but the damages were reduced by 50% for contributory negligence. However, it is comparatively rare for self-harm to be analysed through the prism of the contributory negligence doctrine, since in deliberate self-harm cases the claimant's conduct will usually be regarded as a *novus actus interveniens*, and hence the sole legal cause of the damage.[112]

(b) Causal relevance

2.33 **The claimant's fault must be causally relevant.** Contributory negligence comprises two elements—fault and causation—and both must be present for the doctrine to apply. It follows that the doctrine will not be engaged by causally irrelevant fault. As Lord Atkin said in *Caswell v Powell Duffryn Associated Collieries Ltd*, 'if the plaintiff were negligent but his negligence was not a cause operating to produce the damage there would be no defence'.[113] His Lordship added:[114]

> I find it impossible to divorce any theory of contributory negligence from the concept of causation . . . and whether you ask whose negligence was responsible for the injury, or from whose negligence did the injury result, or adopt any other phrase you please, you must in the ultimate analysis be asking who 'caused' the injury.

Thus, if the damage would have happened even if the claimant had taken reasonable care for his or her own safety or interests a finding of contributory negligence will not be made. For example, in *Beasley v Alexander*, the contributory negligence doctrine was inapplicable because the claimant motorcyclist, even though he had been careless in travelling too quickly, would still have been injured by the defendant's negligence had he been travelling at the 'top safe speed'.[115] Similarly, in *Smith v Finch*,[116] the judge held that the doctrine did not apply because even had the defendant bicyclist worn a helmet it would have made no difference to his injuries.

---

111 [2000] 1 AC 360 (HL). See also the discussion in *Corr v IBC Vehicles Ltd* [2008] UKHL 13, [2008] 1 AC 884.

112 The relationship between the contributory negligence doctrine and the law relating to intervening causes is addressed in 4.02–4.04.

113 [1940] AC 152 (HL) 165.

114 ibid.

115 [2012] EWHC 2197 (QB) [18] (Sir Raymond Jack). See also *Davis v Schrogin* [2006] EWCA Civ 974 [3], [11] (Hughes LJ) (driving more slowly would have made no difference).

116 [2009] EWHC 53 (QB) [54] (Griffith Williams J). To similar effect, see *Phethean-Hubble v Coles* [2011] EWHC 363 (QB) [139]–[140] (HHJ Wilcox).

The requirement of causation has sometimes been misapplied. In *Bowes v The Highland Council*,[117] the court oddly concluded that the defender's negligence in connection with the construction of a bridge rendered causally irrelevant the pursuer's negligent driving even though the driving was a but-for cause of his death. The problem here is that if negligence by the tortfeasor negates the causal relevance of the claimant's fault for the purposes of the contributory negligence doctrine the contributory negligence doctrine will never apply at all. **2.34**

The causation enquiry calls for the application of common sense. It appears that the same principles of causation that apply elsewhere in the law of obligations govern the causation analysis in the contributory negligence context. For example, as is the case in the law of obligations generally, the courts approach causation as a matter of common sense more than anything else. **2.35**

The damage must have been within the scope of the risk created by the claimant's carelessness. It is not enough to engage the contributory negligence doctrine that the claimant's failure to take reasonable care formed part of the background facts. The doctrine will be enlivened only if the damage sustained is within the scope of the risk or risks created by the claimant's lack of reasonable care. In *Jones v Livox Quarries Ltd*,[118] the claimant had been riding on the back of a vehicle when he was crushed after another vehicle struck it from behind. The claimant had failed to take reasonable care for his safety, his negligence had been causative of his injuries, and his damages were reduced as a result. However, no deduction would have been made for contributory negligence, Denning LJ said, if the claimant had instead been shot by a negligent sportsman.[119] That is because the risk of being shot was not within the scope of the risk that the claimant had created by riding on the back of the vehicle. **2.36**

St George v Home Office[120] is a recent illustration of the same principle. In this case, the claimant, who had a long history of alcohol and drug addiction, was sentenced to a term of imprisonment. The prison assigned the claimant a top bunk despite knowing that the claimant was liable to suffer from seizures when in withdrawal. The claimant fell from the bunk as a result of a seizure and suffered injury when he landed on the floor. The plea of contributory negligence failed. Dyson LJ said:[121] **2.37**

> The claimant's fault in becoming addicted to drugs and alcohol in his mid-teens was not a potent cause of the status and the consequent brain injury which were triggered by his fall ... It was too remote in time, place and circumstance and was

---

[117] [2017] CSOH 53 [34] (Lord Mulholland).

[118] [1952] 2 QB 608 (CA).

[119] ibid 616.

[120] [2008] EWCA Civ 1068, [2009] 1 WLR 1670. See also *Calvert v William Hill Credit Ltd* [2008] EWCA Civ 1427, [2009] Ch 330, where it was held (at [70]) that the claimant's having become a compulsive gambler prior to the defendant undertaking a duty of care to him did not amount to contributory negligence, although the claimant was guilty of causally relevant fault in failing to take advantage of 'periods of clarity' after that undertaking to address his addiction.

[121] [2008] EWCA Civ 1068, [2009] 1 WLR 1670 [56].

not sufficiently connected with the negligence of the prison staff... to be properly regarded as a cause of the injury.

2.38 **The claimant's fault must cause the damage but not necessarily the accident.** Although the claimant's fault must be a cause of the damage to amount to contributory negligence, it need not be a cause of the event that led to the claimant being injured. The classic statement of this principle is found in *Froom v Butcher*, a famous seat-belt case. In this case, Lord Denning MR said:[122]

> The question is not what was the cause of the accident. It is rather what was the cause of the damage. In most accidents on the road the bad driving, which causes the accident, also causes the ensuing damage. But in seat belt cases the cause of the accident is one thing. The cause of the damage is another. The *accident* is caused by the bad driving. The *damage* is caused in part by the bad driving of the defendant, and in part by the failure of the plaintiff to wear a seat belt. If the plaintiff was to blame in not wearing a seat belt, the damage is in part the result of his own fault. He must bear some share in the responsibility for the damage ....

2.39 **The claimant's fault need not be a sole cause of the damage and can be causally relevant even if it precedes the defendant's.** Since the question of contributory negligence cannot properly arise unless the defendant is also partly responsible for the damage, it follows that the claimant's negligence need not be a sole cause of the damage. It is enough that it be a cause.[123] Furthermore, the requirement of causal relevance can be satisfied even if the claimant's fault preceded the defendant's.[124]

(3) Responsibility for the Contributory Negligence of Others

2.40 **The doctrine of identification.** One person may be identified with another for various purposes in the law of obligations. In the context of contributory negligence, the doctrine of identification, when applicable, means that the former may be held guilty of contributory negligence on account of the latter's contributory fault.[125] This section offers a bare outline of the relevant law in this regard. Full treatment of this complex subject should be sought elsewhere.

2.41 **Fatal accidents.** Fatal accidents are perhaps the main context in practice in which the doctrine of identification is relevant in relation to contributory negligence. Where a claim is made by dependants in respect of a loss of support under the Fatal Accidents Act 1976, any contributory negligence on the part of the deceased

122 [1976] QB 286 (CA) 292 (emphasis in original).

123 *McLaughlin v Morrison* [2014] CSOH 123, 2014 SLT 862 [12] (Lord Jones).

124 *The Voulte* [1922] 1 AC 129 (HL) 144 (Viscount Birkenhead LC).

125 For discussion, see Charles Gregory, 'Vicarious Responsibility and Contributory Negligence' (1932) 41 Yale Law Journal 831; Malcolm MacIntyre, 'The Rationale of Imputed Negligence' (1944) 5 University of Toronto Law Journal 368.

is attributed to the dependants,[126] and the same is true in respect of claims for bereavement damages.[127]

Congenital injuries. Pursuant to the Congenital Disabilities (Civil Liability) Act 1976, where a child is born disabled due to both the defendant's wrongdoing and the fault of the child's parent, the parent's fault will be imputed to the child and the child's claim against the defendant will thus be subject to the contributory negligence doctrine.[128] **2.42**

Employees. Generally speaking, a claimant will be identified with a third party for the purposes of the law of contributory negligence where the claimant would be vicariously liable for the wrongs of the third party.[129] This approach is often referred to as the 'both ways' test. Suppose that C suffers damage through the combined fault of both D and T. If C is T's employer, T's fault will be imputed to C for the purposes of the contributory negligence analysis in a claim by C against D. Rightly or wrongly, the courts appear to have broadly accepted the idea of vicarious responsibility for contributory negligence as the logical corollary of vicarious liability. **2.43**

Company directors. A company will generally be imputed with the fault of its directors for the purposes of contributory negligence. If those directors delegate their responsibility to other individuals, either within or outside the company, the fault of such individuals will similarly be attributed to the company.[130] **2.44**

Fraud and intentional misconduct. It is unclear to what extent a claimant will be identified with a third party who is an agent, employee, or director of the claimant where the third party has acted fraudulently or has otherwise engaged in intentional misconduct. Treatment of this difficult issue should be sought in more detailed excurses elsewhere.[131] However, it seems likely that in this context the courts will apply the 'both ways' test. A preference in favour of identification can also be expected on the understanding that, as between two innocent parties, it is fairer for the one who employed or otherwise cloaked the fraudster with authority than the one who did not to bear (part of) the loss. **2.45**

Circumstances where the doctrine of identification does not apply. In earlier times, the fault of a driver of a vehicle was attributed to his or her passengers in **2.46**

[126] Fatal Accidents Act 1976, s 5.

[127] ibid s 1A.

[128] The Congenital Disabilities (Civil Liability) Act 1976, s 1(7) provides: 'If in the child's action under this section it is shown that the parent affected shared the responsibility for the child being born disabled, the damages are to be reduced to such extent as the court thinks just and equitable having regard to the extent of the parent's responsibility.'

[129] The law on this point is explored in some detail in PS Atiyah, *Vicarious Liability in the Law of Torts* (Butterworths 1967) 409–14.

[130] *Barings Plc (in liq) v Coopers & Lybrand (a firm)* [2003] EWHC 1319 (Ch), [2003] PNLR 34 [908] (Evans-Lombe J).

[131] The issue is discussed in Andrew Bartlett, 'Attribution of Contributory Negligence: Agents, Company Directors and Fraudsters' (1998) 114 LQR 460; Hugh Evans, 'Attribution and Professional Negligence' (2003) 19 Professional Negligence 470.

certain circumstances.[132] This rule was widely ridiculed and was rejected long ago.[133] Spouses are not identified with each other in this sense,[134] and nor is a child identified with the person in whose care he or she is placed.[135] Accordingly, if a child suffers injury duc to the negligence of both a carer and a third party, the child will not be held guilty of contributory negligence on account of the carer's behaviour in a claim against the third party. Of course, if a third party is sued by a child, the third party may be able to seek contribution from the child's carer.[136] The trend of modern authority is to the effect that a bailor is not identified with his or her bailee's contributory negligence.[137]

[132] *Thorogood v Bryan* (1949) 8 CB 115, 137 ER 452.

[133] *The Bernina* (1888) 13 App Cas 1 (HL).

[134] *Drinkwater v Kimber* [1952] 2 QB 281 (CA).

[135] *Oliver v Birmingham and Midland Motor Omnibus Co Ltd* [1933] 1 KB 35 (KBD).

[136] As in *Jones v Wilkins* [2001] RTR 19 (CA); *Hughes v Williams* [2013] EWCA Civ 455, [2013] PIQR P17.

[137] *Wellwood v King* [1921] 2 IR 290 (CA). See, further, John Fleming, 'Tort Liability for Damage to Hire-Purchase Goods' (1959) 32 Australian Law Journal 267, 273–74.

3

APPORTIONMENT OF RESPONSIBILITY

(1) The Position at Common Law

The common law rule and its demise. At common law, the contributory negligence doctrine functioned as a complete defence: it yielded a verdict for the defendant. It was, in principle, irrelevant that the claimant's share of the responsibility for the damage was small relative to the defendant's. This approach was based on the theory that the claimant's contributory negligence constituted an intervening cause of his or her damage.[1] The draconian nature of this rule prompted the development of several exceptions to it, the best known of which was the 'last opportunity' doctrine. According to that doctrine,[2] the claimant's contributory negligence was disregarded if the defendant had the last opportunity to prevent the damage from being suffered. This network of principles was generally regarded as highly unsatisfactory. It was thought unjust for claimants to be denied recovery altogether on account of comparatively venial fault and, equally, where the 'last opportunity' doctrine (or another exception to the contributory negligence rule) applied, it was considered unfair for the defendant to be made to pay for the entirety of the claimant's damage even though the claimant might have shouldered most of the responsibility for what happened. In addition, the common law was criticized on the basis of its technicality and fine distinctions. This pressure for reform ultimately resulted in the abolition of the all-or-nothing approach and the introduction of the apportionment mechanism. **3.01**

(2) The Apportionment Regime

The apportionment provision. Lying at the heart of the apportionment exercise is section 1(1) of the Law Reform (Contributory Negligence) Act 1945.[3] This provision applies to all parts of the United Kingdom except Northern **3.02**

---

[1] 'Contributory negligence in a plaintiff only means that he himself has contributed to the accident in such a sense as to render the defendant's breach of duty no longer its proximate cause': *Thomas v Quartermaine* (1887) 18 QBD 685 (CA) 694 (Bowen LJ).

[2] The source of this rule is generally considered to be *Davies v Mann* (1842) 10 M & W 546, 152 ER 588.

[3] The 1945 Act is reproduced as Appendix 1. Regarding the Act's history, see Jenny Steele, 'Law Reform (Contributory Negligence) Act 1945: Collisions of a Different Sort' in TT Arvind and

Ireland, although the relevant legislation in that jurisdiction, the Law Reform (Miscellaneous Provisions) Act (Northern Ireland) 1948,[4] contains a materially identical provision, as does legislation in the Crown dependencies.[5] Section 1(1) provides:[6]

> Where any person suffers damage as a result partly of his own fault and partly of the fault of any other person or persons ... the damages recoverable in respect thereof shall be reduced to such extent as the court thinks just and equitable having regard to the claimant's share in the responsibility for the damage.

3.03 **'Fault'**. Section 4 of the 1945 Act states that 'fault' means 'negligence, breach of statutory duty or other act or omission which gives rise to a liability in tort or would, apart from this Act, give rise to the defence of contributory negligence'. In *Standard Chartered Bank v Pakistan National Shipping Corp (Nos 2 and 4)* Lord Hoffmann explained that:[7]

> The definition of 'fault' is divided into two limbs, one of which is applicable to defendants and the other to plaintiffs. In the case of a defendant, fault means 'negligence, breach of statutory duty or other act or omission' which gives rise to a liability in tort. In the case of a plaintiff, it means 'negligence, breach of statutory duty or other act or omission' which gives rise (at common law) to a defence of contributory negligence.

This construction has two consequences. First, the apportionment provision does not apply to causes of action to which the contributory negligence doctrine does not extend, a consequence which can be rationalized on the basis that the purpose of the apportionment provision is to overcome the all-or-nothing rule rather than to prejudice the claimant's recovery in actions to which that rule did not apply. Second, the provision is irrelevant unless and until a finding of contributory negligence is made.[8] That is because the apportionment provision does not empower the court to reduce the claimant's damages on account of conduct on the part of the claimant falling short of 'fault'.[9]

3.04 **'Damage'**. The concept of 'damage' is defined in section 4 of the 1945 Act as including 'loss of life and personal injury'. However, it is clear that for these purposes 'damage' also encompasses property damage and pure economic loss.

Jenny Steele (eds), *Tort Law and the Legislature: Common Law, Statute and the Dynamics of Legal Change* (Hart Publishing 2012).

4 The 1948 Act is reproduced as Appendix 2.

5 Law Reform (Contributory Negligence) Act 1946 (Isle of Man), s 1(1); Law Reform (Miscellaneous Provisions) (Jersey) Law 1960, s 4(1); Law Reform (Tort) (Guernsey) Law 1979, s 1(1).

6 For searching discussion and criticism of s 1(1) see Robert Stevens, 'Should Contributory Negligence be Analogue or Digital?' in Andrew Dyson, James Goudkamp, and Frederick Wilmot-Smith (eds), *Defences in Tort* (Hart Publishing 2015).

7 [2002] UKHL 43, [2003] 1 AC 959 [10].

8 '[A]pportionment only arises where both parties are guilty of negligence': *Cullip v Horsham DC* 1981 WL 687310 (CA) (O'Connor LJ).

9 *Jones v Price* (CA, 1 January 1963).

The effect of the apportionment provision. Where the claimant's 'damage' is caused 'as a result' of the 'fault' of both parties the apportionment provision excludes the common law all-or-nothing rule. The provision also provides that in that event the court[10] 'shall' reduce the recoverable damages. The reduction must be 'just and equitable' bearing in mind the 'claimant's share in the responsibility for the damage'. 3.05

A residual discretion not to reduce damages where there is contributory negligence? Despite the imperative language of the apportionment provision ('shall'), some uncertainty exists as to whether the courts are entitled to refuse to discount the damages once a finding of contributory negligence has been made. There are conflicting judicial statements on this issue. For example, in *Badger v Ministry of Defence*, Stanley Burnton J said: 'Once relevant fault on the part of the claimant has been established, a reduction on account of his fault in the damages recoverable is obligatory.'[11] Conversely, in *Haughton v Patel*, Holroyde J said that even if he had found that the claimant was guilty of contributory negligence, any share she may have had in the responsibility for her own injury would not have justified any reduction in her damages at all.[12] 3.06

Demise of the last opportunity doctrine. After a period of doubt, it was accepted that the apportionment legislation not only excluded the all-or-nothing rule but that it left no room for the much maligned last opportunity doctrine to operate. In 1952, Denning LJ remarked that '[i]t can now be safely asserted that the doctrine of last opportunity is obsolete'.[13] 3.07

Contracting out of the apportionment provision? There is a surprising lack of authority as to whether it is possible to contract out of the apportionment legislation. The statutes provide that they are without prejudice to any defence arising under a contract.[14] This may suggest that it is permissible to contract out of the apportionment regime and back into the all-or-nothing rule.[15] 3.08

(3) Other Apportionment Provisions

Merchant Shipping Act 1995. Section 187 of the Merchant Shipping Act 1995, which is the modern equivalent of section 1 of the Maritime Conventions Act 3.09

[10] And arbitral tribunals: Law Reform (Contributory Negligence) Act 1945, s 4 (defining 'court' to include arbitral tribunals).

[11] [2005] EWHC 2941 (QB), [2006] 3 All ER 173 [15]. See, also, *Boothman v British Northrop Ltd* (1972) 13 KIR 112 (CA) 121–22 (Stephenson LJ) (contending that the apportionment legislation leaves no room for the *de minimis* principle).

[12] [2017] EWHC 2316 (QB) [98]. See, also, *Hawkins v Ian Ross (Castings) Ltd* [1970] 1 All ER 180 (QBD) 188 (Fisher J); *Cullip v Horsham DC* 1981 WL 687310 (CA); *Pankhurst v White* [2006] EWHC 2093 (QB) [22] (Wilkie J).

[13] *Jones v Livox Quarries Ltd* [1952] 2 QB 806 (CA) 615.

[14] Law Reform (Contributory Negligence) Act 1945, s 1(1); Law Reform (Miscellaneous Provisions) (Northern Ireland) Act 1948, s 1(1).

[15] Consider, also, in this regard 4.11 regarding exclusion and limitation clauses or notices.

1911, provides for what are, on their face, somewhat different apportionment rules in cases involving the collisions of ships.[16] Section 187(1) stipulates that:

> Where by the fault of two or more ships, damage or loss is caused to one or more of those ships, to their cargoes or freight, or to any property on board, the liability to make good the damage or loss shall be in proportion to the degree in which each ship was in fault.

Where it is not possible to establish different degrees of fault, responsibility for the damage 'shall be apportioned equally'.[17] However, despite the variations in phrasing, section 187 and the apportionment provision in the 1945 Act are generally to be applied in the same way.[18] The main exception to this seems to be that the courts in proceedings to which section 187 applies tend to ask in apportioning responsibility how many more times at fault one party is relative to the other. Admiralty judges[19] follow Lord Brandon's recommendation that 'it may be found helpful to consider whether the degree of fault of the ship more to blame is one and a half times as great, twice as great, or three, four, five, or even more times as great, as the degree of the fault of the ship less to blame'.[20] This approach is unknown outside the context of section 187.

3.10 **Nuclear Installations Act 1965.** A different regime applies in respect of harm caused by ionizing radiation. Pursuant to section 13 of the Nuclear Installations Act 1965, the amount of compensation due to the claimant is to be reduced 'only if, and to the extent that, the causation of that injury or damage is attributable to the act of the [claimant] committed with the intention of causing harm to any person or property or with reckless disregard for the consequences of his act'.

(4) The Apportionment Exercise Generally

3.11 **The relevant judicial convention.** The apportionment provision does not specify the procedure pursuant to which the appropriate discount is to be determined. The procedure has instead been determined by judicial convention. According to that convention, judges assess the parties' respective shares of responsibility for the damage as two percentages that add up to 100%.[21] The court then reduces

---

16 Full discussion of s 187 and the substantial case law that has sprung up around it is beyond the scope of this volume and should be sought in specialist texts. A leading (albeit dated) analysis of the regime is found in Henry Brandon, 'Apportionment of Liability in British Courts under the Maritime Conventions Act of 1911' (1977) 51 Tulane Law Review 1025.

17 Merchant Shipping Act 1987, s 187(2).

18 *Davies v Swan Motor Co (Swansea) Ltd v James* [1949] 2 KB 291 (CA) 319 (Evershed LJ); *The Miraflores and The Abadesa* [1966] P 18 (CA) 33 (Willmer LJ); *The Nordlake v The Seaeagle* [2015] EWHC 3605 (Admlty), [2016] 1 Lloyd's Rep 656 [145] (Teare J).

19 See, eg, *Samco Europe v MSC Prestige* [2011] EWHC 1580 (Admlty), [2011] 2 Lloyd's Rep 579 [81] (Teare J).

20 Brandon (n 16) 1041.

21 The combined percentages must not exceed 100%: *Black v McCabe* [1964] NI 1 (CA).

the claimant's damages by the percentage of responsibility that it has assigned to him or her.

Apportioning responsibility is a comparative exercise. The apportionment process requires the court to compare the claimant's share of responsibility with that of the defendant. It is impermissible to look at the fault of just one of the parties in isolation from that of the other party. As Hale LJ explained in *Eagle v Chambers*, the apportionment provision 'is premised on both parties being at fault' and, as such:[22] **3.12**

> It is ... impossible to consider the claimant's 'share' [of responsibility] without also considering that of the defendant. Moreover the court has to do what is 'just and equitable' which includes being fair to the claimant as well as to the defendant. Realistically, therefore the court has to compare the one with the other.

Because the apportionment exercise involves comparing the responsibility of both parties, a given act of contributory negligence may attract quite different discounts in different cases depending on the defendant's degree of responsibility. And, in theory, a claimant who is guilty of a minor fault may be lumbered with a larger discount than a claimant who is guilty of more serious negligence, depending on the extent of the defendant's responsibility.

Apportioning responsibility is a discretionary exercise. Apportionment is 'a matter of individual judicial impression'.[23] It has been described as an 'art and not a science'.[24] Indeed, Lord Reed in *Jackson v Murray* said that '[i]t is not possible for a court to arrive at an apportionment which is demonstrably correct'.[25] Nevertheless, the trial judge does not have an 'unfettered discretion'[26] to fix the appropriate discount. As Lord Brandon put it, 'degrees of fault should be established judicially'.[27] **3.13**

Relevance of other cases. The discretionary nature of the apportionment exercise coupled with the fact that it involves a comparison of the parties' respective shares of responsibility means that the discount imposed in any single case is not, in principle, immediately relevant to the discount that should be imposed in another case. Accordingly, judges sometimes remark that being referred to other cases is of 'limited assistance'[28] or 'not ... particularly helpful'[29] because they are **3.14**

---

[22] [2003] EWCA Civ 1107, [2004] RTR 9 [14].

[23] *Hughes-Jukes v Etti* [2006] EWHC 2493 (QB), [2007] RTR 2 [31] (Holland J).

[24] *Powell v Hansen* 2001 WL 753470 (QBD) [131] (Mr Recorder Thorn QC). See also *Adams v Gibson* [2016] EWHC 3209 (QB) [54] (HHJ Freedman) ('not a precise science'). For discussion, see James Goudkamp, 'Apportionment for Contributory Negligence: A Fixed or Discretionary Approach?' (2015) 35 Legal Studies 621.

[25] *Jackson v Murray* [2015] UKSC 5, [2015] 2 All ER 805 [27]. See also at [46] (Lord Hodge).

[26] *Smith v Chief Constable of Nottinghamshire Police* [2012] EWCA Civ 161, [2012] RTR 23 [36] (Ward LJ).

[27] Brandon (n 16) 1032.

[28] *Lightfoot v Go-Ahead Group Plc* [2011] EWHC 89 (QB), [2011] RTR 27 [51] (McCombe J). See also *Jackson v Murray* [2015] UKSC 5, [2015] 2 All ER 805 [50] (Lord Hodge) ('little assistance').

[29] *Sahakian v McDonnell* [2007] EWHC 3242 (QB), [2008] RTR 19 [17] (HHJ Foster QC).

all 'fact-specific'.[30] It has been said that 'it will seldom be appropriate to choose a figure for contributory negligence as between two vehicles in a road traffic accident solely by reference to an assessment in another case, even if that case bears points of similarity with the case under consideration'.[31] Nonetheless, it is common for judges to refer extensively to discounts imposed in other cases,[32] often to reinforce a conclusion to which the judge was already attracted. Christopher Clarke J summarized the approach that the courts take as follows:[33]

> Every case depends on its own facts and limited guidance is to be found in the apportionment determined in other cases with different facts. At the same time, some guidance may be drawn from the approach which the court has taken in cases with features similar to [the proceedings at hand].

3.15 **Number of faults.** It is common to see judges tallying up the number of faults on both sides with a view to ascertaining the proper apportionment of responsibility.[34] The impression is sometimes created that the party who is guilty of more faults will be assigned with a larger share of the responsibility for the damage. However, it is clear that the apportionment exercise should not be reduced to keeping a tally. As Sir Gordon Willmer said in *The Koningin Juliana*, 'apportionment of blame in the Admiralty Court is not to be arrived at by totting up and comparing the number of faults in the navigation of each vessel ... The inquiry must be qualitative rather than quantitative. It is necessary to look at the over-all picture.'[35] These remarks were made in the context of the predecessor to section 187 of the Merchant Shipping Act 1995[36] but they apply to the apportionment process more generally.

3.16 **Contributory negligence preceding the defendant's fault.** Just as a claimant can be adjudged guilty of contributory negligence based on conduct that precedes the defendant's wrongdoing,[37] there is no rule that the court cannot consider conduct on the part of the claimant that precedes the defendant's fault in apportioning responsibility. Where the liability is grounded on a relationship between the parties (eg as in most professional negligence cases), the court will 'look at the whole picture from the start of the [parties'] relationship'.[38]

3.17 **Counter-claims.** For example, if C's vehicle collides with D's and both parties are at fault, a counter-claim may well be brought. Where this happens, both parties are likely to be found guilty of contributory negligence. The apportionment in the initial claim will almost certainly be the mirror image of the apportionment

---

[30] *Tavares v Hudson-Rotin* [2012] EWHC 3171 (QB) [49] (Globe J).
[31] *Wagner v Grant* [2016] CSIH 34, 2016 SLT 699 [40] (Lord Menzies).
[32] See, eg, *Lunt v Khelifa* 2001 WL 1479700 (QBD); *McCreery v Letson* [2015] CSOH 153 [78] (Lord Bannatyne); *Buck v Ainslie* [2017] CSOH 73 [99]–[103] (Lady Carmichael).
[33] *Toropdar v D* [2009] EWHC 2997 (TCC) [16] (Christopher Clarke J).
[34] See, eg, *Bruma v Hassan* [2017] EWHC 3209 (QB) [72]–[73] (HHJ Curran QC).
[35] [1974] 2 Lloyd's Rep 353 (CA) 364.
[36] See 3.09.
[37] See 2.39.
[38] *Lloyds Bank Plc v McBains Cooper Consulting Ltd* [2018] EWCA Civ 452 [40] (Longmore LJ).

in the counter-claim. Thus, if the claimant is held to be 75% responsible for the damage for the purposes of the claim against the defendant, then the defendant will very likely be held to be 25% responsible for the damage in the counter-claim. In *Eagle v Chambers*, Hale LJ (with whom Ward and Waller LJJ concurred) said that:[39]

> [T]he arithmetic will reflect the different amounts of damage done. Thus, while one might not wish to rule out the possibility that there might be an exceptional case in which different apportionments were possible, no one has yet thought of an example where this would be so.

(5) The Criteria of Apportionment

The twin criteria. In *Stapley v Gypsum Mines Ltd*, Lord Reid said:[40] **3.18**

> A court must deal broadly with the problem of apportionment and in considering what is just and equitable must have regard to the blameworthiness of each party, but 'the claimant's share in the responsibility for the damage' cannot, I think, be assessed without considering the relative importance of his acts in causing the damage apart from his blameworthiness.

The need to consider these two factors has been repeatedly confirmed, including by Lord Reid himself nearly two decades later in *Baker v Willoughby*, where he said: 'There are two elements in an assessment of liability, causation and blameworthiness.'[41] In addressing these twin criteria, it is necessary for the court to consider all of the relevant circumstances of the case.[42]

The twin criteria are flexible tools. In *Corr v IBC Vehicles Ltd*, Lord Walker said **3.19**
that they 'are not precise or mutually exclusive tests'.[43] Similarly, in *Rehill v Rider Holdings Ltd*, Richards LJ observed that 'it [is] difficult to draw a clear distinction between [them]'.[44] Underscoring the fact that the line between the two criteria is unclear, in *Jackson v Murray* Lord Reed accepted that a given factor may relate to both criteria and said that 'the overall assessment of responsibility should not be affected by the heading under which [a] factor is taken into account'.[45]

Relative blameworthiness. The courts have not fully explained the idea of rela- **3.20**
tive blameworthiness. However, this criterion seems to focus on how far below the standard of the reasonable person each party fell. It appears that the parties' respective ages are relevant when it comes to considering relative blameworthiness. For example, in *Scutts v Keyse*, HHJ Hutton said 'it is particularly important

[39] [2003] EWCA Civ 1107, [2004] RTR 9 [15].
[40] [1953] AC 663 (HL) 682.
[41] [1970] AC 467 (HL) 490.
[42] *Toropdar v D* [2009] EWHC 2997 (TCC) [40] (Christopher Clarke J).
[43] [2008] UKHL 13, [2008] 1 AC 884.
[44] [2012] EWCA Civ 628, [2013] RTR 5 [30].
[45] [2015] UKSC 5, [2015] 2 All ER 805 [40].

to bear in mind the youth and relative inexperience of [the claimant], a young man ... not yet 18, [and] the considerable experience and much greater age of the [defendant] police driver'.[46]

3.21 **Causal potency.**[47] The law regarding the causal potency criterion is underdeveloped. On one view it is little more than a screen behind which judges can impose the discount they think justice requires. However, the case law suggests that the conduct of the party who created the danger that materialized will often be regarded as being more causally potent.[48] Furthermore, motorists are usually treated as playing a more causally potent role in bringing about damage than pedestrians on account of the significant destructive potential of motor vehicles.[49] Serious debate can be had about the sense of the causal potency criterion. In particular, it is unclear whether it is coherent to say that it is even possible for one cause to be more potent than another. It is worth noting that no room is made in Canada for the causal potency criterion.

3.22 **Additional criteria?** It is unclear whether the twin criteria of relative blameworthiness and causal potency are the only factors that the courts take into account in determining the appropriate apportionment of responsibility. In *Reeves v Commissioner of Police of the Metropolis,* the deceased, who was of sound mind, committed suicide while in police custody. The police were in breach of the duty of care that they owed the deceased to safeguard him from self-harm. Lord Hoffmann said: 'The apportionment must recognise that a purpose of the duty accepted by the commissioner in this case is to demonstrate publicly that the police do have a responsibility for taking reasonable care to prevent prisoners from committing suicide.'[50] Lord Hoffmann did not say, however, whether this factor was relevant in its own right, or because it went to one or both of relative blameworthiness and causal potency.

3.23 One interesting question is whether it is permissible to consider in the apportionment exercise only those acts of the claimant that have been held to constitute contributory negligence in the first place. Suppose, for example, that the defendant alleges two acts of contributory negligence, but that the court makes a finding of contributory negligence in respect only of the first act, on the grounds that the second act, although careless, was not causally relevant. Is it permissible for the court to take the claimant's second act of carelessness into account in its decision on apportionment despite its not comprising contributory negligence? The same issue can be posed in relation to the defendant's conduct. In

[46] 2000 WL 33201536 (QBD). Consider also *Eagle v Chambers* [2003] EWCA Civ 1107, [2004] RTR 9 [18] (Hale LJ).

[47] For further discussion of the causal potency criterion, see James Goudkamp and Lewis Klar, 'Apportionment of Damages for Contributory Negligence: The Causal Potency Principle' (2016) 53 Alberta Law Review 1.

[48] *Samco Europe v MSC Prestige* [2011] EWHC 1580 (Admlty), [2011] 2 Lloyd's Rep 579 [84] (Teare J); *Sabir v Osei-Kwabena* [2015] EWCA Civ 1213 [16] (Tomlinson LJ).

[49] *Sinclair v Joyner* [2015] EWHC 1800 (QB) [73] (Cox J); *Sabir v Osei-Kwabena* [2015] EWCA Civ 1213 [16] (Tomlinson LJ).

[50] [2000] 1 AC 360 (HL) 372.

apportioning responsibility must the court consider only those acts of the defendant that rendered the defendant liable to the claimant? The law on this point is unclear. The broad-brush approach that the courts take to the apportionment canvas[51] suggests that the entirety of both parties' conduct is material. Arguably, however, the apportionment legislation requires a different approach as it stipulates that only responsibility for damage caused by 'fault' is to be apportioned, and the term 'fault' means either the conduct that renders the defendant liable or the conduct that constitutes contributory negligence.[52]

(6) Discounts Imposed

Empirical data. According to empirical research into first instance decisions in England and Wales, the average discount by which damages are reduced for contributory negligence across all types of claim is 40%.[53] The average discount by contextual category was found to be as follows: road accident (42%), employers' liability (31%), occupiers' liability (51%), professional negligence (58%), public liability (39%), sports injury (38%), and miscellaneous (37%). **3.24**

Broad-brush approach. Consistently with the fact that the apportionment exercise is discretionary and that it does not admit of a demonstrably correct answer,[54] the courts take a broad-brush approach to apportionment and tend to reduce the claimant's damages either by the fractions used most frequently in everyday life (such as one-half, one-quarter, and one-third) or by percentages that are multiples of 10 (10%, 20%, etc).[55] Judges[56] strive not to become 'bogged down by fine-shadings of percentages'.[57] **3.25**

Very low and very high discounts. Discounts that fall at the extremes of the spectrum cast doubt on whether the contributory negligence doctrine is properly applicable in the first place. A discount of, say, 5% suggests that the claimant's contribution to the damage is so miniscule that the claimant is not, in reality, guilty of contributory negligence. Similarly, a finding of 95% contributory negligence suggests that the claimant is wholly responsible for the damage and that the defendant ought not to be held liable at all. The practice of the courts is broadly consistent with these propositions. Thus, discounts of less than 10% are **3.26**

[51] See 3.13.

[52] See 3.03.

[53] James Goudkamp and Donal Nolan, 'Contributory Negligence in the Twenty-First Century: An Empirical Study of First Instance Decisions' (2016) 79 MLR 575.

[54] See 3.13.

[55] See further Goudkamp and Nolan (n 53) 598–99 (by far the most frequently observed discount in first instance cases was 50%, followed by 33.3% and 25%).

[56] Juries sometimes proceed differently. In a New Zealand case, *Joll v Watson* [1953] NZLR 788 (SC), a jury reduced the claimant's damages by 52%. And in a recent Scottish case, a jury reduced the pursuer's damages by 96.5%: see https://www.scotcourts.gov.uk/about-the-scottish-court-service/scs-news/2017/05/09/first-civil-jury-trial-for-all-scotland-sheriff-personal-injury-court (accessed 31 December 2017).

[57] *Powell v Hasen* 2001 WL 753470 (QBD) [131] (Mr Recorder Thorn QC).

unusual.[58] In *Cooper v Carillion Plc*, Keane LJ said that '[t]he issue in this case, given the low figure of 10 per cent attributed by the judge in respect of the claimant's contributory negligence, is whether the judge was right to find that there was contributory negligence at all on the part of the claimant'.[59] Discounts approaching 100% are also rare. In *Hodkinson v Henry Wallwork & Co Ltd*,[60] the damages of an employee who took an 'amazing risk' in an attempt to fix a machine were reduced by 90%. In *Barings Plc (in liq) v Coopers & Lybrand (a firm)*,[61] the judge would have discounted damages by 95% in respect of conduct committed over a certain given period of time had he found that primary negligence had remained operative. For a time, the courts insisted, irrationally, that it was possible to reduce damages by 100%.[62] However, that view has rightly been repudiated and the courts have confirmed that such a discount is not permitted under the apportionment regime.[63] In a recent empirical study of first instance decisions on contributory negligence from England and Wales, the lowest discount imposed was 10%, and the highest was 90% (apart, that is, from two discounts of 100%, which are now revealed to have been impermissible).[64]

3.27 **Different discounts in respect of different time periods.** Where the conduct constituting contributory negligence is carried out over a long duration, different apportionments of responsibility can apply in respect of different periods of time. For example, in *Barings Plc (in liq) v Coopers & Lybrand (a firm)*,[65] Evans-Lombe J fixed the claimant's responsibility at 50%, 60%, and 80% in relation to three temporal windows spread over around eighteen months.

3.28 **Guideline discounts.**[66] In *Froom v Butcher*,[67] Lord Denning MR famously promulgated guideline discounts in seat-belt cases. He did so on the basis that

---

58 But see *Pasternack v Poulton* [1973] 1 WLR 476 (QBD) (5%); *Snushall v Fulsang* (2006) 258 DLR (4th) 425 (Ont CA) (5%); *Nominal Defendant v Rooskov* [2012] NSWCA 43, (2012) 60 MVR 350 (5%). See also the discussion (see 3.06) regarding whether the courts have a discretion not to reduce the claimant's damages where contributory negligence has been established.

59 [2003] EWCA Civ 1811 [11]. Consider also Sedley LJ's remark in *Butcher v Cornwall CC* [2002] EWCA Civ 1640 [13] that '10% is so nearly a token figure that one's first reaction is that it betokens an absence of significant fault on the claimant's part'.

60 *Hodkinson v Henry Wallwork & Co Ltd* [1955] 3 All ER 236 (CA).

61 [2003] EWHC 1319 (Ch) [1068] (Evans-Lombe J).

62 *Imperial Chemical Industries Ltd v Shatwell* [1965] AC 656 (HL) 672 (Lord Reid); *McMullen v National Coal Board* [1982] ICR 148 (QBD) 154–55 (Caulfield J); *Jayes v IMI (Kynoch) Ltd* [1985] ICR 155 (CA) 159 (Robert Goff LJ); *McEwan v Lothian Buses Plc* [2006] CSOH 56, 2006 SCLR 592 [32]–[35] (Lord Emslie); *Byron Avenue* [2010] NZCA 65, [2010] 3 NZLR 445 [63] (Baragwanath J).

63 *Wynbergen v Hoyts Corp Pty Ltd* (1997) 72 ALJR 65 (HCA); *Anderson v Newham College of Further Education* [2002] EWCA Civ 505, [2003] ICR 212 [19] (Sedley LJ); *Buyukardicli v Hammerson UK Properties Plc* [2002] EWCA Civ 683 [7] (Sedley LJ).

64 Goudkamp and Nolan (n 53) 598–99.

65 [2003] EWHC 1319 (Ch) [1069].

66 See, generally, Goudkamp (n 24).

67 [1976] QB 286 (CA) (noted in JR Spencer, 'Belt Up!—The Widening Scope of Contributory Negligence' (1976) 35 CLJ 44).

guidelines would save the cost of enquiring as to the individual circumstances of each and every seat-belt case. According to his Lordship:[68]

> Sometimes the evidence will show that the failure [to wear a seat belt] made no difference. The damage would have been the same, even if a seat belt had been worn. In such case the damages should not be reduced at all. At other times the evidence will show that the failure made all the difference. The damage would have been prevented altogether if a seat belt had been worn. In such cases I would suggest that the damages should be reduced by 25 per cent. But often enough the evidence will only show that the failure made a considerable difference. Some injuries to the head, for instance, would have been a good deal less severe if a seat belt had been worn, but there would still have been some injury to the head. In such case I would suggest that the damages attributable to the failure to wear a seat belt should be reduced by 15 per cent.

The courts rarely depart from these guidelines.[69] In *Capps v Miller*, Croom-Johnson LJ said that '[o]ne does not say that they should never be departed from, but ordinarily they should be adhered to'.[70] The defendant carries the onus of showing that the guidelines should not be applied,[71] which onus will be discharged only where the case is 'rare or exceptional'.[72] The guidelines were not followed in *Hazlett v Robinson*, where the judge found that had a seat belt been used, the damage would have been 'very [much] less severe',[73] and imposed a discount of 20%. Nor were they followed in *Bennett v Brinks Ltd*,[74] in which the defendant employer condoned the failure by the claimant employee to wear a seat belt, and the damages were reduced by only 10%.

When *Froom* was decided, it was compulsory for cars to be fitted with seat belts **3.29** but not mandatory to wear them. Consequently, upon its becoming mandatory to use seat belts in cars, it was thought that the *Froom* guidelines might need to be revisited, and *Froom* has thus been challenged on several occasions. However, those challenges have been forcefully rejected,[75] and it appears that the courts have little appetite for reconsidering *Froom*. On the contrary, the *Froom* guidelines have been extended to contribution proceedings where a parent negligently failed properly to secure their infant child in their vehicle.[76] They have also been extended beyond the seat-belt context to failures by motorcyclists[77]

---

68 [1976] QB 286 (CA) 296.

69 Examples of cases in which *Froom* was followed include *Patience v Andrew* [1983] RTR 447 (QBD); *Gawler v Raettig* [2007] EWHC 373 (QB); *Palmer v Kitley* [2008] EWHC 2819 (QB); *Mabiriizi v HSBC Insurance (UK) Ltd* [2011] EWHC 1280 (QB) [10] (Sharpe J).

70 [1989] 1 WLR 839 (CA) 849.

71 *Stanton v Collinson* [2009] EWHC 342 (QB) [140] (Cox J).

72 *Gawler v Raettig* [2007] EWHC 373 (QB) [26] (Gray J).

73 [2014] NIQB 17 [53] (Gillen J).

74 [1999] CLY 1378 (Leeds CC).

75 *Gawler v Raettig* [2007] EWHC 373 (QB) [39]–[46] (Gray J); *Stanton v Collinson* [2010] EWCA Civ 81, [2010] RTR 26 [26] (Hughes LJ).

76 *Jones v Wilkins* [2001] RTR 19 (CA) [13]–[14] (parent liable for 25% of the damages); *Hughes v Williams* [2013] EWCA Civ 455, [2013] PIQR P17 (same).

77 'I see no reason to distinguish between seat belt cases and crash helmet cases and I would apply the dictum of Lord Denning to crash helmets just as he spoke of it in seat belts': *Capps v*

and bicyclists[78] to wear crash helmets,[79] although it is less clear whether they are closely adhered to in those settings,[80] partly because there have been relatively few recent cases involving a failure to wear a helmet.

3.30 Conversely, the *Froom* guidelines were not followed in a case in which the claimant suffered injury while riding in the boot of a car.[81] Nor were the guidelines followed in a case in which a coach passenger failed to wear a seat belt, with the judge placing weight on the fact that it was not then compulsory to wear a seat belt on coaches and on the fact that there was no educational campaign by the government at the relevant time to encourage persons travelling by coach to use seat belts.[82] The courts have made little effort to formulate guidelines pitched at different levels from those in *Froom*. In *Best v Smyth*, Tugendhat J wrote that since *Owens v Brimmell*[83] 'the figure of 20% is commonly regarded as the appropriate reduction for a claimant who has got into a vehicle when he must have known that the driver had had too much to drink'.[84] However, it is doubtful whether the courts adhere closely to that prescription.[85]

(7) Children

3.31 According to empirical research, the average discount in the case of adults is 39%, whereas the average for children is 43%.[86] This result is slightly unexpected and, together with the fact that children are more likely to be found guilty of contributory negligence,[87] casts significant doubt on the accuracy of the commonly expressed perception that courts treat children more leniently than adults when it

Miller [1989] 1 WLR 839 (CA) 847 (Croom-Johnson LJ). It appears that the *Froom* guidelines were followed by agreement in *McCracken v Smith* [2013] EWHC 3620 (QB) [83] (Keith J), in which the claimant pillion passenger failed to wear a helmet (15%).

[78] 'In my judgment the observations of Lord Denning MR … should apply to the wearing of helmets by cyclists': *Smith v Finch* [2009] EWHC 53 (QB) [44] (Griffith Williams J). Contra *Sinclair v Joyner* [2015] EWHC 1800 (QB) [71], in which Cox J doubted whether failing to wear a helmet while riding a bicycle amounted to contributory negligence, although it is not entirely clear whether she was speaking generally or only in the context of that case.

[79] For discussion, see Julian Fulbrook, 'Cycle Helmets and Contributory Negligence' [2004] Journal of Personal Injury Law 171.

[80] Consider *Malasi v Ahmed* [2011] EWHC 4083 (QB) (80%); *Reynolds v Strutt & Parker LLP* [2011] EWHC 2263 (QB) (66.6%); *McCracken v Smith* [2013] EWHC 3620 (QB) (45%). See also *Perrin v Ministry of Defence* [2001] EWCA Civ 1310 (20%), which is a helmet case but not in a road accident context.

[81] *Gleeson v Court* [2007] EWHC 2397 (QB), [2008] RTR 10 [25] (HHJ Foster QC).

[82] *Welsh v Messenger* [2006] CLY 2875 (Newcastle upon Tyne CC).

[83] [1977] QB 859 (QBD).

[84] [2010] EWHC 1541 (QB) [12].

[85] Consider, eg, *Currie v Clamp* 2002 SLT 196 (OH) (33.3%).

[86] Goudkamp and Nolan (n 53) 603.

[87] See 2.18.

comes to the application of the contributory negligence doctrine.[88] One explanation for it is that in practice judges are not, contrary to authority, applying an age-relative standard of care to child claimants,[89] but holding them to an adult standard. Another explanation is that children (or perhaps more specifically teenagers) are less risk averse than adults, and so tend to take less care of their own safety.

(8) Strict Liability

The apportionment exercise is sometimes thought to be rendered more complex or even confounded altogether where the obligation that the defendant breached was one of strict liability. The concern seems to be that it is impossible to compare the parties' respective shares of responsibility where the defendant is strictly liable. However, this view is affected by serious confusion. For one thing, although strict liability is liability irrespective of fault, a defendant who is held strictly liable will often have been at fault. Furthermore, when the apportionment legislation applies, the court is required to assign shares of responsibility to the parties, and a party can be responsible (in the sense of that word that matters for the purposes of the apportionment legislation) without being at fault. As much is clear from the fact that the apportionment exercise involves consideration not only of the parties' relative blameworthiness but also of the relative causative potency of their conduct. As Lord Hoffmann observed in *Reeves v Commissioner of Police of the Metropolis*, '[a] person may be responsible although he has not been careless at all, as in the case of breach of an absolute statutory duty'.[90] **3.32**

(9) Criminal Conduct

Just as participating in criminal conduct will often amount to contributory negligence,[91] so too will such participation tend to be highly relevant for the purposes of the apportionment exercise. As Edis J explained in *Hicks v Young*, '[t]hat is because criminal or reckless conduct is morally more blameworthy than conduct which is merely careless'.[92] *McCracken v Smith*[93] is a good illustration of a case in which criminal conduct by the claimant was highly relevant to the apportionment exercise. In that case, a pillion passenger on a trail bike was injured in an accident for which the defendant minibus driver was partly responsible. The parties agreed that a 15% discount was warranted on account of the claimant's **3.33**

---

[88] 'The courts have been singularly lenient to children both in terms of finding them guilty of contributory negligence and in apportioning damages': Caroline Sappideen and Prue Vines (eds), *Fleming's The Law of Torts* (10th edn, Thomson Reuters Professional (Australia) Ltd 2011) 330.

[89] See 2.16.

[90] [2000] 1 AC 360 (HL) 371.

[91] See 2.31.

[92] [2015] EWHC 1144 (QB) [35].

[93] [2013] EWHC 3620 (QB).

failure to wear a helmet. However, other acts of contributory negligence, which included the fact that the claimant had allowed himself to be carried as a pillion passenger when he knew that this was not permitted, and also that the bike's driver was unlicensed and uninsured, led the court to impose a total discount of 45%.[94] In *Groves v Studley*,[95] the claimant threatened the defendant driver and jumped onto the bonnet of his car, whereupon the defendant accelerated and swerved, causing the claimant to fall from the vehicle and suffer injury. Damages were reduced by 40%.

(10) Professional Negligence

3.34 Empirical evidence suggests that, in general, it is particularly difficult to establish that the claimant is guilty of contributory negligence in professional negligence cases.[96] However, according to this research when the plea of contributory negligence succeeds, the average discount tends to be high. In the study in question, the average discount in professional negligence claims at first instance was considerably higher (58%) than the average discount across all first instance claims (40%). One possible explanation for this inverse relationship between the success rate of the plea of contributory negligence and the average discount is that claimants need to do something particularly unreasonable in order to be found guilty of contributory negligence in the professional negligence setting. If this is correct, then judges may conclude that claimants who have been found guilty of contributory negligence in the professional negligence context deserve to have their damages discounted by a sizeable amount. Another possible explanation for the relatively high discounts in professional negligence cases is that in other types of case, such as road accident claims, considerations of causative potency play a greater role in the apportionment decision, whereas in professional negligence claims the focus is often exclusively on the relative fault of the parties, and this more often leads to the conclusion that an equal division of responsibility is appropriate.

3.35 High discounts for contributory negligence can be expected in the professional negligence setting where the claimant's fault is independent of that of the defendant (in that it does not lie in not checking or verifying the professional's work), or where the thing that the claimant ought to have done, or which the claimant failed properly to do, did not require technical competence. A good example of a case in which the claimant's fault was independent of that of the defendant is *Sahib Foods Ltd v Paskin KyriaKides Sands (a firm)*,[97] a case concerning fire damage to the claimant's factory, where liability was imposed on the defendant architects for the inadequate fireproofing of a food preparation room, but the damages were reduced by 66.6% because the claimant's employees had both caused the fire and contributed to its spreading by misinforming the

[94] ibid [83] (Keith J).
[95] [2014] EWHC 1522 (QB).
[96] See 2.26.
[97] [2003] EWCA Civ 1832, [2004] PNLR 22.

defendants about the nature of the cooking process involved. Similarly, in *Logical Computer Supplies Ltd v Euro Car Parks Ltd*,[98] the compensation awarded to a company for damage to its computer files that had been caused by employees of an IT firm hired to supply an email system was reduced by 50% on account of the company's failure to apply 'business common sense and risk management'[99] by properly backing up its data.

(11) Aggravating Factors

The following circumstances tend to inflate the discount. 3.36

The claimant was experienced in the activity in question. The discount will tend to be increased where the claimant had significant experience in the activity in question. For example, in *Ringe v Eden Springs (UK) Ltd*,[100] the court emphasized that the claimant was an experienced motorcyclist who was familiar with the road, and with the type of traffic that usually travelled on it, in deciding to impose a discount of 80% on account of his riding too quickly and overtaking in a manner that was unsafe. In *Causby v Seagoe Technologies Ltd*, the claimant suffered injuries at work. In determining the discount for the claimant's contributory negligence in the manner in which he had unloaded pallets, McCloskey J attached significance to his 'experience in the activity in question'.[101] 3.37

The claimant was aware of the risk of injury. Where the claimant was subjectively aware of the danger that led to his or her being injured this will tend to lead to a higher discount. For example, in *Russell v West Sussex CC*,[102] the judge placed weight on the fact that the claimant driver knew that the road was slippery on account of the presence of frost but did not modify her speed as a result. Similarly, the fact that the claimant was given but did not heed a warning regarding the risk that materialized will also tend to weigh in the defendant's favour.[103] 3.38

The claimant was driving or riding too quickly. A paradigmatic aggravating factor is driving or riding too quickly in all of the circumstances. It is routine for judges to take travelling at too high a speed into account in fixing the discount, and significant weight will often be attached to it.[104] This factor tends to inflate 3.39

---

98 2001 WL 825094 (QBD).

99 ibid [14] (Richard Fernyhough QC).

100 [2012] EWHC 14 (QB).

101 [2009] NIQB 24. See also *Hicks v British Transport Commission* [1958] 1 WLR 493 (CA) (50%) (experienced shunter); *Akel v Havering LBC* 1999 WL 982477 (CA) (experienced gym user) (50%); *Stephen v Peter* 2005 Rep LR 53 (CSOH) [38] (Lord Menzies) (90%) (experienced lorry driver); *Sandison v Coope* 2016 Rep LR 70 (Tayside, Central and Fife Sheriff Court) (experienced bicyclist) (30%).

102 [2009] EWHC 1063 (QB) (50%).

103 See, eg, *Eagle v Chambers* [2003] EWCA Civ 1107, [2004] RTR 9 [18] (Hale LJ) (40%).

104 See, eg, *Buchan v Whiting* [2009] EWHC 2951 (QB) [42]–[44] (Blake J) (50%); *Train v Secretary of State for Defence* [2014] EWHC 1928 (QB) (80%); *Buswell v The Motor Insurers Bureau* [2015] EWHC 1379 (QB) [54] (Supperstone J) (66.6%).

the discount even when the claimant was travelling below or around the speed limit but nonetheless faster than was safe in the circumstances.[105]

3.40 **The claimant crossed a road diagonally.** Judges regularly place weight on the fact that the claimant was crossing a road diagonally. Crossing a road in this way is presumably treated as an aggravating factor[106] because the claimant is exposed to the risk of being struck by oncoming traffic for longer.

3.41 **The claimant was wearing dark clothing at night.** Judges routinely attach significance in road accident cases to the fact that a claimant pedestrian was wearing dark clothing at night, and hence was more difficult for motorists to observe.[107] It appears that this consideration goes only to causal potency rather than to relative blameworthiness.[108] Conversely, the fact that the claimant was wearing light-coloured clothing at night may operate in his or her favour.[109]

3.42 **Failure to use a nearby pedestrian crossing.** Judges often emphasize the fact that a claimant pedestrian struck by a vehicle failed to use a nearby pedestrian crossing.[110]

3.43 **Intoxication.** Judges regularly place significant weight on the fact that the claimant was intoxicated at the time of the accident.[111] On the other hand, the mere fact that the claimant was intoxicated will not count against him or her, since it is only causally relevant fault that matters for the purposes of the contributory negligence doctrine.[112] According to Lord Boyd in *Smith v Bluebird Buses Ltd*, '[t]he critical issue is not whether [the pursuer] was under the influence of alcohol but what his actions were'.[113] Similarly, judges have sometimes remarked that the fact of intoxication by itself is unimportant for the purposes of

105 See, eg, *Jones v Lawton* [2013] EWHC 4108 (QB) [44] (Burnett J) (33.3%).

106 See, eg, *Kane v New Forest Council* 2001 WL 1903436 (QBD) (33.3%); *Markowski v Elson* [2001] CLY 4477 (Weymouth CC) (33.3%); *Lightfoot v Go-Ahead Group Plc* [2011] EWHC 89 (QB), [2011] RTR 27 [40] (McCombe J); *Smith v Bluebird Buses Ltd* [2014] CSOH 75, 2014 Rep LR 91 [27] (Lord Boyd) (85%).

107 See, eg, *Scutt v Keyse* 2000 WL 33201536 (QBD) (25%); *Lunt v Khelifa* 2001 WL 1479700 (QBD) (33.3%); *Carpenter v Lunnon* [2004] EWHC 3079 (QB) [62]–[63] (Mr Anthony Temple QC) (20%); *Callier v Deacon* [2009] EWHC 245 (QB) [26] (HHJ McKenna) (55%); *Bruma v Hassan* [2017] EWHC 3209 (QB) [73] (HHJ Curran QC) (20%).

108 *Carpenter v Lunnon* [2004] EWHC 3079 (QB) [63] (20%).

109 Consider *Eagle v Chambers* [2003] EWCA Civ 1107, [2004] RTR 9 [17] (Hale LJ) (40%).

110 *McDermott v Pettit* [2011] EWHC 3074 (QB) [31], [40] (Parker J) (10%); *Smith v Bluebird Buses Ltd* [2014] CSOH 75, 2014 Rep LR 91 [26], [29] (Lord Boyd) (85%); *Adams v Gibson* [2016] EWHC 3209 (QB) [46] (HHJ Freedman) (33.3%); *Bruma v Hassan* [2017] EWHC 3209 (QB) [73] (HHJ Curran QC) (20%); cf *White v Chapman* 2001 WL 825325 (QBD) [12] (HHJ Wilkie QC) (claimant not guilty of contributory negligence in failing to use pelican crossing that was 35 metres away, although at fault in crossing where no refuge was available); *Crew v Ash* [2008] EWHC 3068 (QB) [28] (Lloyd Jones J) (claimant not guilty of contributory negligence in failing to cross at a light-controlled crossing that was only 'metres' away).

111 See, eg, *Barrett v Ministry of Defence* [1995] 1 WLR 1217 (CA) (66.6%); *McCaughey v Mullan* [2014] NIQB 132 [16] (O'Hara J) (60%).

112 *Lightfoot v Go-Ahead Group Plc* [2011] EWHC 89 (QB), [2011] RTR 27 [38] (McCombe J).

113 [2014] CSOH 75, 2014 Rep LR 91 [26] (Lord Boyd) (85%).

the apportionment exercise because intoxication 'merely ... serves to explain why [the claimant] failed to take proper care for his own safety'.[114]

Proceeding against a red light. In *Rehill v Rider Holdings Ltd*, Richards LJ referred to the fact that the claimant had crossed at 'a controlled pedestrian crossing with the red man showing against pedestrians'.[115] His Lordship continued: 'That was a strong reason in itself why the claimant should not have attempted to cross at all. If he was minded to attempt to cross despite the red light, it was plainly incumbent on him to check very carefully indeed on the state of the traffic.'[116] Richards LJ concluded that the claimant's conduct was 'seriously blameworthy' and he increased the discount of 33.3% that had been imposed at first instance to 50%. In *Malasi v Ahmed*, the claimant cyclist ran a red light and was struck by a taxi. The judge said that 'the balance of fault' lay 'very heavily' with the claimant because 'had [he] not chosen to disregard a red traffic signal, he would not have exposed himself to the risks of those circumstances which have eventuated'.[117] 3.44

Failure by the claimant to keep a proper lookout. A classic aggravating factor is failing to keep a proper lookout for danger. This factor tends to be particularly relevant in road accident cases where brief moments of inattention can have catastrophic consequences.[118] Judges regularly remark, in particular, that pedestrians are expected to look both ways before entering the carriageway.[119] Even a claimant who uses a designated crossing area may still be expected to keep a lookout for oncoming traffic. For example, in *Clifford v Drymond*,[120] the claimant, who was using a zebra crossing, failed to keep an approaching vehicle under observation. Her damages were reduced by 20%, although it has been suggested that the case might be decided differently today.[121] It has also been said that claimants who walk on the road should walk facing oncoming traffic.[122] 3.45

The claimant became distracted or was otherwise paying insufficient attention. The fact that the claimant permitted himself or herself to become distracted will tend to enlarge the discount. For example, in fixing the appropriate discount, judges have taken account of the fact that the claimant's attention was on 3.46

[114] *McNab v Bluebird Buses Ltd* [2007] CSOH 36 [11] (Lord Brodie); *Lightfoot v Go-Ahead Group Plc* [2011] EWHC 89 (QB), [2011] RTR 27 [39] (McCombe J); *Adams v Gibson* [2016] EWHC 3209 (QB) [48] (HHJ Freedman).

[115] [2012] EWCA Civ 628, [2013] RTR 5 (50%).

[116] ibid [31].

[117] [2011] EWHC 4083 (QB) [28] (HHJ Seymour QC) (80%).

[118] See, eg, *Jones v Lawton* [2013] EWHC 4108 (QB) [44] (Burnett J); *McAllister v Campbell* [2014] NIQB 24 [21] (Stephens J); *Wagner v Grant* [2015] CSOH 51 [17] (Lord Uist).

[119] See, eg, *Honnor v Lewis* [2005] EWHC 747 (QB) [52], [63] (Silber J) (20%); *Ehrari v Curry* [2006] EWHC 1319 (QB) [11] (Jack J) (70%); *Adams v Gibson* [2016] EWHC 3209 (QB) [46] (HHJ Freedman) (33.3%).

[120] [1976] RTR 134 (CA).

[121] *Sabir v Osei-Kwabena* [2015] EWCA Civ 1213 [17] (Tomlinson LJ).

[122] *Carpenter v Lunnon* [2004] EWHC 3079 (QB) [62] (Mr Anthony Temple QC) (20%); *McNab v Bluebird Buses Ltd* [2007] CSOH 36 [11] (Lord Brodie) (50%).

a mobile telephone,[123] a heart-rate monitor,[124] and the rear wheel of a bicycle in front of the claimant's.[125]

(12) Mitigating Factors

3.47 The following circumstances tend to reduce the discount.

3.48 **Vulnerability of the claimant.** The susceptibility of the claimant to injury is often cited as a powerful mitigating consideration. For example, in *Powell v Hansen*,[126] Mr Recorder Thorn QC placed weight on the fact that, as a motorcyclist, the claimant belonged to a class of person especially prone to suffer serious injury.[127] And in *Jones v Lawton*, Burnett J said that the vulnerability of the claimant motorcyclist in terms of causative potency 'tilt[ed] the balance decisively in [his] favour'.[128] Similarly, it is widely acknowledged that pedestrians are particularly vulnerable to being injured by vehicles and that this factor usually tilts the apportionment exercise in their favour. For example, in *McCreery v Letson*, Lord Bannatyne said: 'it is clear from the case law that in a road traffic case one factor which should be had regard to is the potential destructive disparity between the pedestrian and the person driving the vehicle'.[129] In *Jackson v Murray*, Lord Reed identified this consideration as a factor to be taken 'into account when assessing blameworthiness', although he added that 'the overall assessment of responsibility should not be affected by the heading under which' it was taken into consideration.[130] In *Eagle v Chambers,* Hale LJ said '[i]t is rare indeed for a pedestrian to be found more responsible than a driver unless the pedestrian has suddenly moved into the path of an oncoming vehicle',[131] and in *Lunt v Khelifa* Latham LJ said that the law 'has consistently imposed on the drivers of cars a high burden to reflect the fact that a car is potentially a dangerous weapon'.[132]

3.49 **The claimant's conduct was socially beneficial.** The courts sometimes emphasize that allowances should be made for the fact that the claimant, when injured, was engaged in some socially worthwhile activity, or doing something that was required by his or her employment. For example, in *Gilfillan v Barbour,* Lord Reed took into account in the claimant's favour the fact that the claimant, although

[123] *Joseph v Braid* 2003 Rep LR 133 (OH) [60] (Lord Bracadale) (66.6%).

[124] *McAllister v Campbell* [2014] NIQB 24 [9], [21] (Stephens J) (25%).

[125] *Daly v Heeps* 2018 GWD 2-45 (Lothian and Borders Sheriff Court) [36] (Sheriff Peter J Braid) (50%).

[126] 2001 WL 753470 (QBD) [128] (20%).

[127] See also the remarks in *McAllister v Campbell* [2014] NIQB 24 [21] (Stephens J) (bicyclist); *McGeer v McIntosh* [2017] EWCA Civ 79 [28] (Treacy LJ) (bicyclist).

[128] [2013] EWHC 4108 (QB) [44].

[129] [2015] CSOH 153 [76] (50%).

[130] [2015] UKSC 5, [2015] 2 All ER 805 [40] (50%).

[131] [2003] EWCA Civ 1107, [2004] RTR 9 [16] (40%). See also *Smith v Bluebird Buses Ltd* [2014] CSOH 75, 2014 Rep LR 91 [28] (Lord Boyd) (85%). This approach is not limited to cars but has been extended to motorcycles: *Greenwood v Cummings* (QBD, 9 April 2008).

[132] [2002] EWCA Civ 801 [20].

he was driving 'much too fast in the circumstances', was fulfilling his duties as a police officer at the time.[133]

The claimant had priority. In road traffic cases, the fact that the claimant had priority (for example, because he or she was on the more major road) will tend to lead to a lower discount where the defendant failed to give way and an accident then occurred.[134] The position will be otherwise where it was the defendant who had priority, which the claimant failed to respect.[135] 3.50

The defendant's negligence created the danger. Where the claimant did not create the risky situation, but merely reacted to an emergency that was brought about by the defendant's negligence, the courts will often assign the bulk of the responsibility for the damage to the defendant. Thus, where the defendant motorist negligently pulled in front of the claimant's vehicle and the claimant's reaction was inadequate, the defendant will typically be held to have been primarily responsible.[136] In *The Miraflores and The Abadesa*, Lord Pearce said:[137] 3.51

> It is axiomatic that a person who embarks on a deliberate act of negligence should, in general, bear a greater degree of fault than one who fails to cope adequately with the resulting crisis which is thus thrust upon him. This generality is subject, of course, to the particular facts. And it may be that the initial act was so slight or easily avoidable and the subsequent failure to take avoiding action so gross that the blame for the accident falls more largely or even (if the interval and opportunity for avoidance are sufficiently great) wholly upon the person who failed to avoid the consequences of another's negligence. Between the extremes in which a man is either wholly excused for a foolish act done in the agony of the moment as the result of another's negligence or is wholly to blame because he had plenty of opportunity to avoid it, lies a wide area where his proportion of fault in failing to react properly to a crisis thrust upon him by another must be assessed as a question of degree. But the driver who deliberately goes round a corner on the wrong side should, as a rule, find himself more harshly judged than the negligent driver who fails to react promptly enough to the unexpected problem thereby created. For all humans can refrain from deliberately breaking well-known safety rules; but 'tis not in mortals to command the perfect reaction to a crisis, and many fall short at times of that degree which reasonable care demands.

The claimant was walking rather than running. In pedestrian cases, the courts generally look sympathetically on claimants who were proceeding slowly across a road.[138] This approach is doubtless because slower-moving pedestrians usually 3.52

---

133 2003 SLT 1127 (OH) [40] (50%).

134 See, eg, *Nicolson v Willis* [2006] EWHC 2402 (QB) [49] (Sir John Blofeld).

135 *Joseph v Braid* 2003 Rep LR 133 (OH) [61] (Lord Bracadale) (66.6%); *Flavio v Jeffrey* [2008] EWHC 2331 (QB) [13] (Mackay J) (66.6%); *Armsden v Kent Police* [2009] EWCA Civ 631, [2009] RTR 31 [24] (Stanley Burnton LJ) (60%).

136 See *Jones v Lawton* [2013] EWHC 4108 (QB) [44] (Burnett J) (33.3%). See also *Nicolson v Willis* [2006] EWHC 2402 (QB) [51] (Sir John Blofeld) (33.3%); *Rickson v Bhakar* [2017] EWHC 264 (QB) [32] (Blake J) (20%).

137 [1967] 1 AC 826 (HL) 847–48.

138 See, eg, *Sedge v Prime* [2011] EWHC 820 (QB) [37] (HHJ Burrell QC) (25%); *Bruma v Hassan* [2017] EWHC 3209 (QB) [72] (HHJ Curran QC) (20%).

afford drivers a greater opportunity to take evasive measures. Conversely, claimants who are injured while darting out suddenly into the carriageway tend to have their damages discounted by larger amounts.[139] If, however, the claimant is already part of the way across the road and breaks into a run in order to avoid being struck by an oncoming vehicle, the court may regard that as a mitigating factor.[140]

3.53 **Pedestrian activity in the area was likely.** Extra care is required of defendant motorists when passing through an area where nearby facilities (such as schools, bus stops, and underground stations) suggest that pedestrian activity is likely.[141] Thus, the mere fact that the area was 'built up' or 'shop-lined' tends to work in the claimant's favour,[142] as does the presence of parked cars[143] and a stationary minibus that has its hazard lights activated.[144]

3.54 **The claimant had nearly reached the other side of the road.** If the claimant had crossed most of the roadway before being struck by an oncoming car, a lower discount can be expected than if the claimant had been hit while close to the kerb from which they set off.[145] That is because where a pedestrian has almost made it to the other side of the road, a driver is likely to have had a greater opportunity to observe and avoid the pedestrian.

3.55 **The claimant was placed under pressure by the defendant.** Where the claimant engaged in the conduct that amounted to contributory negligence at the defendant's urging, that will tend to diminish the discount, especially if the defendant was in a position of responsibility relative to the claimant.[146]

(13) Types of Damages Amenable to Reduction

3.56 **The term 'damages' is undefined in the apportionment legislation.** In the vast majority of cases in which the contributory negligence doctrine is in issue only compensatory damages will have been awarded, and these can of course be reduced for contributory negligence. However, the situation is less clear in relation to certain other types of damages, such as punitive damages and aggravated damages. The apportionment statutes give little by way of guidance in this regard as

139 See, eg, *Paramasivan v Wicks* [2013] EWCA Civ 262 (75%).

140 *Hickman v London Central Bus Co Ltd* [2013] EWHC 1703 (QB) [66], [69] (Sir Robert Nelson) (40%); cf *Hughes-Jukes v Etti* [2006] EWHC 2493 (QB), [2007] RTR 2 [30] (Holland J) (30%).

141 See, eg, *Eagle v Chambers* [2003] EWCA Civ 1107, [2004] RTR 9 [17] (40%) (Hale LJ); *Bruma v Hassan* [2017] EWHC 3209 (QB) [72] (HHJ Curran QC) (20%).

142 See, eg, *Bruma v Hassan* [2017] EWHC 3209 (QB) [72] (HHJ Curran QC) (20%); *Sabir v Osei-Kwabena* [2015] EWCA Civ 1213 [13], [16] (Tomlinson LJ) (25%).

143 See, eg, *Brownlow v Knight* [2003] NIQB 71 [18] (Campbell LJ) (40%).

144 *Jackson v Murray* [2015] UKSC 5, [2015] 2 All ER 805.

145 See, eg, *Honnor v Lewis* [2005] EWHC 747 (QB) [60] (Silber J) (20%).

146 See, eg, *Ministry of Defence v Radclyffe* [2009] EWCA Civ 635 (40%).

they say only that the recoverable 'damages' shall be reduced where there is contributory negligence, but leave the term 'damages' undefined.

Punitive damages. Virtually no case law exists regarding the interaction of the contributory negligence doctrine and the law governing punitive damages. This is unsurprising given that the jurisdiction to award punitive damages will generally not be exercised where the claimant is partly to blame for what happened.[147] In *Ali v Hartley Poynton Ltd*,[148] where punitive damages were awarded, the judge assumed that only compensatory damages were amenable to reduction for contributory negligence. However, according to Michael Tilbury and Harold Luntz, the apportionment legislation is 'capable of encompassing exemplary damages'.[149] The Law Commission of England and Wales was more hesitant on this issue, but nevertheless observed that it was arguable that the apportionment statutes applied to awards of punitive damages.[150] The better view seems to be that the legislation does not permit the court to discount punitive damages. It is important in this regard to observe that reductions in the claimant's 'damages' under the apportionment provision are determined by reference to the parties' respective shares 'in the responsibility for the damage'. In the context of the statute, it could be argued that the term 'damage' refers to the claimant's loss.[151] That understanding would strongly suggest that the 'damages' to which the apportionment provision refers are those relating to the claimant's loss. Those 'damages' are compensatory damages, not punitive damages. Another argument in favour of this view is that the purpose of punitive damages is to punish the defendant, and they are set accordingly. Once the court has arrived at a sum deemed appropriate for the punishment of the defendant, there is no reason to reduce that sum to reflect the claimant's partial responsibility for the damage he or she suffered. 3.57

Aggravated damages. There is slender authority as to whether aggravated damages are amenable to reduction for contributory negligence, and cases which raise this issue are likely to be rare. However, given that (unlike punitive damages) aggravated damages are compensatory in nature,[152] there is in principle no reason why aggravated damages should not be reduced by reference to the claimant's contributory negligence. 3.58

[147] *Thompson v Commissioner of Police of the Metropolis* [1998] QB 498 (CA) 518 (Lord Woolf MR).

[148] [2002] VSC 113, [2002] Aust Torts Reports 81-665.

[149] Michael Tilbury and Harold Luntz, 'Punitive Damages in Australian Law' (1995) 17 Loyola of Los Angeles International & Comparative Law Journal 769, 790.

[150] Law Commission, *Aggravated, Exemplary and Restitutionary Damages* (Law Com No 247, 1997) 81n.

[151] But see *Drinkwater v Kimber* [1952] 2 QB 281 (CA).

[152] Aggravated damages 'are primarily to be awarded to compensate the plaintiff for injury to his proper pride and dignity and the consequences of his being humiliated': *Thompson v Commissioner of the Police of the Metropolis* [1998] QB 498 (CA) 512 (Lord Woolf MR).

(14) Multiple Parties

3.59 **Multiple defendants.** Where two or more defendants are liable for the same damage, they will be treated as a single defendant for the purposes of the apportionment exercise.[153] Thus, if C is injured by D1 and D2, C's share of the responsibility will be ascertained prior to any assessment of D1 and D2's shares of responsibility *inter se*, which assessment will be relevant only for the purposes of any claim in contribution.

3.60 **Multiple claimants.** Where there are two claimants, the damages recoverable by each may be subject to different discounts. Nonetheless, it is not uncommon for the courts to assign to claimants who are working in collaboration with, or are otherwise related to, each other the same percentage of responsibility for the damage.[154]

3.61 **Position where not all of the wrongdoers are party to the proceedings.** The apportionment legislation may require the court to consider the fault of wrongdoers who are not parties to the proceedings.[155] Thus, if C suffers damage due to the wrongs of both D1 and D2, as well as C's own carelessness, and C sues only D1, in determining C's share of responsibility for the damage it is necessary to take account of D2's fault. However, the judgment of the court in this regard will not, of course, bind D2.

---

[153] *Fitzgerald v Lane* [1989] AC 328 (HL).

[154] See, eg, *Trebor Bassett Holdings Ltd v ADT Fire and Security Plc* [2011] EWHC 1936 (TCC) (both claimants assigned 75% of the responsibility for the damage); *Khan v Harrow LBC* [2013] EWHC 2687 (TCC), [2013] BLR 611 (both claimants assigned 15% of the responsibility for the damage).

[155] *The Nordlake v The Seaeagle* [2015] EWHC 3605 (Admlty), [2016] 1 Lloyd's Rep 656 [146] (Teare J).

4

RELATED RULES

The fact that the claimant failed to take reasonable care for his or her own safety or interests may be relevant to rules other than the contributory negligence doctrine. No fewer than eight other areas of law may be identified in this regard. They are: (i) the principles governing intervening causation; (ii) the '*SAAMCO* cap'; (iii) the illegality doctrine; (iv) the voluntary assumption of risk principle; (v) exclusion or limitation of liability clauses or notices; (vi) the doctrine of mitigation of damage; (vii) the doctrine of provocation; and (viii) the compensatory principle. It is reasonably common for certain of these other rules to be relied upon simultaneously with the law of contributory negligence, especially the illegality doctrine and the voluntary assumption of risk principle.[1] This section considers the distinctions between these eight areas of law on the one hand and the law of contributory negligence on the other. Also closely related to the law of contributory negligence is the doctrine of contribution between wrongdoers. Like the principles governing contributory negligence, the law regarding contribution provides for the apportionment of responsibility.[2] However, in contrast with the former, the latter is concerned not with apportioning responsibility between wrongdoer and victim but between wrongdoers *inter se*. Accordingly, because the doctrine of contribution does not affect the claimant's recovery, unlike all of the other rules discussed in this section, it is not considered here. **4.01**

(1) Intervening Causation

Contributory negligence can constitute an intervening cause. Where the claimant's contributory negligence plays a sufficiently significant role in bringing about his or her damage it may constitute an intervening cause of that damage. Where that happens, the claim will usually fail in its entirety, and there will be no room for the law of contributory negligence to operate. Exceptionally, however, the intervening cause analysis will render only a particular item of loss irrecoverable, as opposed to defeating the claim altogether.[3] Such an outcome is **4.02**

[1] See, eg, *Berry v Hayden* [2008] NIQB 134.
[2] Civil Liability (Contribution) Act 1978, s 2.
[3] See, eg, *McKew v Holland & Hannen & Cubitts (Scotland)* [1969] 3 All ER 1621 (HL).

conceptually distinct from the type of partial recovery that the law of contributory negligence yields since recovery in respect of the full amount of the individual loss concerned will be denied.

4.03 **The claimant's conduct must obliterate the defendant's wrongdoing.** The law that determines when the claimant's conduct will amount to an intervening cause as opposed to mere contributory negligence is 'imprecise'.[4] However, in principle, an intervening cause analysis applies only where the claimant's conduct is such that 'it obliterates the wrongdoing of the defendant'.[5] For this to be the case, it has been said that the claimant's conduct must be 'reckless or worse than reckless',[6] although on other occasions it has been held that recklessness is not required.[7] The leading case of *McKew v Holland & Hannen & Cubitts (Scotland)*[8] illustrates these principles.[9] The defender negligently injured the pursuer, who later fell down a staircase which he should not have tried to descend without assistance in view of his injuries. The pursuer sustained further injury in the fall. It was held that the defender was not liable for the injuries caused by the fall because the pursuer's fault in descending the stairs was an intervening cause of the damage. Lord Reid said:[10]

> [I]f the injured man acts unreasonably he cannot hold the defender liable for injury caused by his own unreasonable conduct. His unreasonable conduct is novus actus interveniens. The chain of causation has been broken and what follows must be regarded as caused by his own conduct and not by the defender's fault or the disability caused by it.

4.04 **Defendant's fault led to the claimant engaging in the conduct concerned.** The case will not be analysed as one involving intervening causation where the defendant was under a duty to prevent the conduct of the claimant in question. In *Bhatt v Fontain Motors Ltd*, the claimant employee fell from a ladder in the defendant employer's car showroom. The defendant breached a statutory duty that required work at height to be avoided altogether if it was reasonably practicable to carry out the work otherwise than at height. Richards LJ said:[11]

---

4 *Hicks v Young* [2015] EWHC 1144 (QB) [44] (Edis J).

5 *Stephen v Peter* 2005 Rep LR 53 (CSOH) [36] (Lord Menzies).

6 *Clift v Hawes* 1999 WL 1457275 (CA) (Sedley LJ).

7 'In my judgment there does not have to be recklessness and nothing less than recklessness ...': *Lambert v Lewis* [1982] AC 225 (CA) 252 (Roskill LJ) (reversed on other grounds on appeal). According to Peter Cane, '[r]ecklessness in its core sense is commonly conceptualised in terms of awareness of a risk that certain consequences will result from conduct, and indifference to that risk ... A person is reckless in relation to a particular consequence of their conduct if they realise that their conduct may have that consequence, but go ahead anyway. The risk must have been an unreasonable one to take ...': Peter Cane, '*Mens Rea* in Tort Law' (2000) 20 OJLS 533, 535 (footnote omitted).

8 [1969] 3 All ER 1621 (HL).

9 See also *Quinn v Burth Bros (Builders) Ltd* [1966] 2 QB 370 (CA); *Spencer v Wincanton Holdings Ltd* [2009] EWCA Civ 1404, [2010] PIQR P8.

10 [1969] 3 All ER 1621 (HL) 1623.

11 [2010] EWCA Civ 863, [2010] PIQR P17 [34]. See also *Neil v East Ayrshire Council* 2005 Rep LR 18 (OH) [27]–[29] (Lord Brodie).

> [The claimant's] failure to follow the prescribed procedure when doing work he should not have been required to do at all, and when using equipment that he should not have been required to use if the work was to be done, does not mean that the accident was caused by him alone. It goes only to contributory negligence.

This principle applies even where the claimant engaged in deliberate self-harm and was of sound mind at the relevant time.[12]

(2) The *SAAMCO* Cap

The so-called '*SAAMCO* cap'[13] is part of the law of remoteness of damage. It dictates that a defendant is liable only for loss or damage that it was his or her duty to prevent. Suppose, for example, that a lender suffers loss because the value of security that it holds is insufficient to discharge the liability of a defaulting borrower, because the property that constitutes the security was negligently over-valued. Applying the *SAAMCO* cap, the maximum liability of the valuer will be limited to the difference between the actual value of the property when it was valued and the valuation given. The valuer will not be responsible for other losses that the lender may suffer due to entering into the transaction, such as losses incurred as a result of having to sell the property at an inopportune time. Suppose, for example, that A lends B £900,000 to purchase property which is valued at £1m but worth only £500,000 and that B defaults. The valuer's liability will be capped at £500,000. The valuer will not be liable for £900,000 because that is the sum lost by A as a result, for example, of the property being destroyed in a fire. **4.05**

Any discount to the claimant's damages on account of his or her contributory negligence falls to be made before the *SAAMCO* cap is applied.[14] It is convenient to illustrate what this means by elaborating upon the scenario in the previous paragraph. Suppose that A was guilty of contributory negligence in the order of 25% because A should have realized that B would be unable to service the loan. The actual loss suffered by A is £900,000. The claim in respect of that loss would be reduced by 25% to £675,000. However, because that sum exceeds the loss for which the valuer is liable (ie £500,000), the lender's recovery will in fact be unaffected by its contributory negligence. **4.06**

(3) Reasonable Reliance and the Principle in *Hedley Byrne & Co Ltd v Heller & Partners Ltd*

In order for a duty of care to arise pursuant to the principle in *Hedley Byrne & Co Ltd v Heller & Partners Ltd*,[15] the claimant must, according to traditional **4.07**

[12] *Reeves v Commissioner of Police of the Metropolis* [2000] 1 AC 360 (HL). See 2.32.

[13] After the decision in *South Australia Asset Management Corp v York Montague Ltd* [1997] AC 191 (HL).

[14] *Platform Home Loans v Oyston Shipways* [2000] 2 AC 190 (HL).

[15] [1964] AC 465 (HL).

doctrine, rely on the defendant's assumption of responsibility,[16] and that reliance must be reasonable.[17] It follows that where the claimant has been careless in relying on an assumption of responsibility, a duty of care will not arise on the principle in *Hedley Byrne*. Of course, if a duty of care arises because the reliance was reasonable, that does not exclude the possibility that the claimant will have been careless with respect to his or her own interests in some other way. Where that occurs, the claimant's recovery will be reduced for contributory negligence despite the dependency of the claimant's cause of action on the rule established by *Hedley Byrne*.

(4) Illegality

4.08 The relationship between the illegality and contributory negligence doctrines is complex, not least because the law governing the former has undergone significant development lately,[18] and the full implications of those developments have not yet been worked out.[19] A claimant's contributory negligence may constitute a criminal offence and hence also trigger the illegality doctrine (*ex turpi causa non oritur actio*). Similarly, illegal conduct is likely, where causally relevant, to amount to contributory negligence. Accordingly, it is entirely possible for a given course of conduct by the claimant to be material to both the doctrines of illegality and contributory negligence. Where that occurs, the claimant's cause of action as a whole will fail on account of the illegality, unless the illegality affects only a specific head of damages, such as damages for a loss of earnings.[20] The point was specifically addressed in *Vellino v Chief Constable of Greater Manchester*.[21] In that case, the claimant threw himself out of a second-floor window to avoid being arrested by the police. The claimant sued in negligence in respect of the police officers' failure to restrain him. Sedley LJ, dissenting, suggested that the apportionment legislation may have ousted not only the common law rule that contributory negligence was fatal to the claimant's cause of action, but the illegality doctrine too.[22] However, that view was not accepted by the majority, which rejected the claim on account of the claimant's illegal conduct.[23] Finally, it should be noted that trivial offending does not enliven the illegality doctrine,[24] whereas

16 *Henderson v Merrett Syndicates Ltd* [1995] 2 AC 145 (HL) 194 (Lord Goff) ('an assumption of responsibility coupled with the concomitant reliance may give rise to a tortious duty of care').

17 *Berry v Taylor (a firm) v Coleman* [1997] PNLR 1 (CA) 1 (Staughton LJ).

18 See *Patel v Mirza* [2016] UKSC 42, [2017] AC 467 (noted in James Goudkamp, 'The End of an Era? Illegality in Private Law in the Supreme Court' (2017) 133 LQR 14).

19 For a conspectus of the law, see James Goudkamp, 'The Law of Illegality After *Patel v Mirza*: Identifying the Issues' in Alan Bogg and Sarah Green (eds), *Illegality After* Patel v Mirza (Hart Publishing 2018).

20 See *Burns v Edman* [1970] 2 QB 541 (QBD); James Goudkamp and Lorenz Köing, 'Illegal Earnings' (2018) 9 Journal of European Tort Law 54.

21 [2001] EWCA Civ 1249, [2002] 1 WLR 218.

22 ibid [54].

23 ibid [34] (Schiemann LJ), [71]–[72] (Sir Murray Stuart Smith).

24 *Les Laboratoires Servier v Apotex Inc* [2014] UKSC 55, [2015] AC 430 [29] (Lord Sumption).

minor wrongdoing routinely constitutes contributory negligence. For example, a failure to wear a seat belt or driving a little in excess of the speed limit is dealt with exclusively by the law of contributory negligence.

(5) Voluntary Assumption of Risk

The voluntary assumption of risk doctrine (*volenti non fit injuria*) applies where a claimant consented to the lack of reasonable care that created the risk of injury that materialized.[25] In these circumstances, the claimant's cause of action will fail in its entirety. Prior to the enactment of the apportionment legislation, there was little reason rigorously to distinguish between the voluntary assumption of risk and contributory negligence doctrines, as both operated as a complete defence to the claim. However, following the adoption of apportionment for contributory defence, the distinction is highly pertinent, since although voluntary assumption of risk continues to defeat the claim altogether, contributory negligence now operates only to reduce the damages payable. **4.09**

It is widely thought that the availability of apportionment for contributory negligence has contributed to the decline of the voluntary assumption of risk doctrine. For example, in 1964 Lord Reid said that 'in most cases where the [voluntary assumption of risk doctrine] would ... be available it has become usual to base the decision on contributory negligence'.[26] Similarly, Lord Denning MR said in 1971 that '[n]ow that contributory negligence is not a complete defence, but only a ground for reducing the damages, the defence of volenti non fit injuria has been closely considered, and, in consequence, it has been severely limited'.[27] Today, few claims fail on the ground that the claimant was *volens* to the risk of injury,[28] and many of the cases that use the language of voluntary assumption of risk seem to be using that terminology to express the conclusion that there was no breach of duty or no causal link between any breach and the claimant's damage.[29] One final point to note about the relationship between the two doctrines is that although the voluntary assumption of risk doctrine applies only where the claimant is subjectively aware of the risk concerned,[30] the law of contributory negligence turns on an objective test.[31] **4.10**

---

25 *Wooldridge v Sumner* [1963] 2 QB 43 (CA) 69 (Diplock LJ).

26 *Imperial Chemical Industries Ltd v Shatwell* [1965] AC 656 (HL) 672.

27 *Nettleship v Weston* [1971] 2 QB 691 (CA) 701.

28 But see *Morris v Murray* [1991] 2 QB 6 (CA).

29 For discussion, see James Goudkamp, *Tort Law Defences* (Hart Publishing 2013) 55–58, 60, 70, 74.

30 *Bartlett v The English Cricket Board Association of Cricket Officials* 2015 WL 5037730 (Wolverhampton CC) [55] (HHJ Lopez) ('*Volenti* has no application as the Claimant has not perceived there is a risk'); *Lear v Hickstead Ltd* [2016] EWHC 528 (QB), [2016] 4 WLR 73 [101] (Picken J) ('[the claimant] was unaware of the risk of the ramp falling on him. He cannot, therefore, be regarded as having voluntarily accepted the risk that what happened to him would happen').

31 See 2.15.

(6) Exclusion and Limitation Clauses or Notices

4.11 Contractual provisions or notices that exclude or limit the defendant's liability are given effect according to their proper interpretation unless they are rendered unenforceable by statute.[32] One interesting question that arises in connection with exclusion or limitation clauses or notices is whether they fall to be applied before or after the contributory negligence doctrine. Suppose that D contracts with C that, in the event that C has a claim against D, D's damages will be capped at £1m. And suppose that C has a claim against D in respect of a loss of £1.5m, but that C is guilty of contributory negligence, which is held to merit a 50% deduction in his damages. In such a case, is C entitled to damages of £500,000 or £750,000? The courts have not given a clear answer to this question. However, arguably, any limitation of liability clause falls to be applied first (unless the clause expressly or by necessary implication provides otherwise) and the contributory negligence doctrine second. The result is that, absent provision to the contrary in the contract, when both a limitation of liability clause and the defence of contributory negligence apply, damages are capped at the agreed limit and then discounted for contributory negligence. This approach is supportable on the basis that the apportionment statutes operate to reduce 'the damages *recoverable*'. It thus seems that the legislation does not extend to damage that is irrecoverable, such as on account of a limitation of liability clause. Furthermore, several authorities indirectly support the view that limitation of liability clauses fall to be applied prior to the contributory negligence defence. In *Kelly v Stockport Corp*,[33] a claim was brought in a court whose jurisdiction was limited to £200, with the claimant claiming that maximum figure. The trial judge found that the claim was worth £300 but that the claimant was guilty of contributory negligence sufficient to warrant reducing the damages by one-third. On appeal, it was unanimously held that the claimant could recover only £133 (being two-thirds of £200) rather than £200 (being two-thirds of £300). The reasoning was that the discount is to be applied to the 'damages recoverable', as per the statutory language of section 1 of the 1945 Act, and that the jurisdictional limit of the court meant that the claimant could not recover more than £200. There is clearly a powerful analogy to be drawn between a jurisdictional cap on the damages that can be awarded and a limitation of liability clause with the result that, by parity of reasoning, a limitation of liability clause falls to be applied before the contributory negligence defence.

(7) Mitigation of Damage

4.12 The law concerning mitigation of damage comprises three central principles. First, there is the rule that a claimant cannot hold the defendant accountable for damage that the claimant could have avoided by taking reasonable care. For

[32] Unfair Contract Terms Act 1977, Pt 1; Consumer Rights Act 2015, Pt 2.
[33] [1949] 1 All ER 893 (CA).

example, if a claimant unreasonably fails to undergo treatment for an injury the claimant will be unable to recover compensation in respect of losses that would have been avoided had the treatment been given. A second rule permits the claimant to charge the cost of reasonable efforts taken in mitigation of his or her damage to the defendant. These costs are chargeable regardless of whether they are successful in reducing the claimant's damage (indeed, they are chargeable even if they worsen the claimant's situation). Third, a claimant cannot recover damages to the extent that he or she has avoided loss resulting from the defendant's wrong irrespective of whether the steps taken were ones that were reasonably required of the claimant.

The precise nature of the relationship between the law of contributory negligence and the law of mitigation of damage is problematic.[34] According to one view, the former is concerned with pre-tort fault whereas the latter relates to post-tort fault.[35] However, this distinction is not free from difficulty: for one thing, cases can be found in which conduct occurring after the tort was held to constitute contributory negligence.[36] As for the substance and effect of the two doctrines, there are both similarities and differences. The most obvious similarity is that both doctrines are governed by objective tests, in that they are concerned with the reasonableness of what the claimant did. Conversely, two distinctions between the two doctrines should also be highlighted. One is that contributory negligence results only in the claimant's recovery being scaled back, whereas a claimant who fails to mitigate his or her damage cannot recover in respect of any of that damage: the right to recover under particular heads of damage may be eliminated entirely and, indeed, exceptionally, a claim may fail completely. And the other is that the law of mitigation of damage, but not the law of contributory negligence, can increase the claimant's recoverable loss, as where the claimant reasonably but unsuccessfully incurs expenditure with a view to reducing his or her damage. **4.13**

(8) Provocation

When applicable, the doctrine of provocation diminishes awards of punitive damages.[37] There is some support for the proposition that the doctrine is also **4.14**

[34] It is considered at length in Iain Field, 'Contributory Negligence and the Rule of Avoidable Losses' (2018) OJLS (forthcoming).

[35] See, eg, James Edelman et al, *McGregor on Damages* (20th edn, Sweet & Maxwell 2017) para 6-018 ('Distinguishing between the application of contributory negligence and that of mitigation is comparatively easy. In this context, contributory negligence comes in only before the commission of the wrong, mitigation necessarily after its commission').

[36] See, eg, *The Calliope* [1970] P 172 (Probate, Divorce and Admlty Div); *Berry v Calderdale Health Authority* 1998 WL 1043808 (CA); *Spencer v Wincanton Holdings Ltd* [2009] EWCA Civ 1404, [2010] PIQR P8.

[37] *Fontin v Katapodis* (1962) 108 CLR 177 (HCA); *Lane v Holloway* [1968] 1 QB 379 (CA); *Hoebergen v Koppens* [1974] 2 NZLR 597 (SC).

capable of reducing compensatory damages.[38] There is clearly a certain parallel between the law of contributory negligence and the rules regarding provocation, and indeed, several scholars take the view that the doctrine of provocation is a specific application of the doctrine of contributory negligence. For instance, Lewis Klar claims that:[39]

> Contributory negligence can be defined as any unreasonable conduct on the part of a plaintiff which contributes to his injury. Provocation can be viewed as a specific type of contributorily negligent behaviour. [Reliance on both doctrines involves the defendant] arguing that the plaintiff's provocatory conduct was unreasonable and contributed to his own injury.

Likewise, David Cheifetz writes that 'the doctrine of provocation ... seems suspiciously like contributory fault'.[40] He concludes 'that the doctrine of provocation in relation to intentional torts is in fact a restatement of contributory fault'[41] and that 'provocation is flagrant contributory fault—something more than mere carelessness for one's own safety'.[42]

4.15 However, and contrary to the foregoing, the doctrines of contributory negligence and provocation are separate from each other. Whereas contributory negligence by definition involves fault on the part of the claimant, it is doubtful whether provocation requires the claimant to have been at fault.[43] For example, a defendant may claim to have been provoked by a claimant who, because of a mental illness from which he or she suffers, would not be considered to be at fault for the purposes of a contributory negligence analysis.[44] Furthermore, the doctrine of provocation, unlike the doctrine of contributory negligence, seems to require close scrutiny of the quality of the defendant's response. No parallel enquiries are made in asking whether the claimant is guilty of contributory negligence. Because of these fundamental differences between the doctrines of contributory negligence and provocation the better view is that the latter is not a subspecies of the former.

---

[38] *Hurley v Moore* (1993) 112 Nfld & PEIR 40 (CA); *Murphy v Culhane* [1977] QB 94 (CA) 98 (Lord Denning MR); *McAleer v Chief Constable of the PSNI* [2014] NIQB 53 [28] (Gillen J); *Rennie v Morrison* [2014] CSOH 123, 2014 SLT 862 [17] (Lord Jones).

[39] Lewis Klar, 'Recent Developments in Canadian Law: Tort Law' (1985) 17 Ottawa Law Review 325, 336–37.

[40] David Cheifetz, *Apportionment of Fault in Tort* (Canada Law Book Ltd 1981) 197.

[41] ibid 197–98.

[42] ibid 199.

[43] For an extreme example from the criminal law, see *R v Doughty* (1986) 83 Cr App R 319 (CA) (provocation consisted in the incessant crying of a 17-day-old baby). cf Lord Jones's remark in *Rennie v Morrison* [2014] CSOH 123, 2014 SLT 862 [17] that 'the act of provocation must be a wrongful act, otherwise an entirely innocent act which happens to anger an irrational wrongdoer would operate to exclude or mitigate damages for injury caused by the irrational wrongdoer's unlawful act'.

[44] See 2.19.

(9) Compensatory Principle

The compensatory principle—the rule that the successful claimant is entitled to damages that put the claimant into the position that he or she would have been in but for the defendant's breach of duty—requires extensive predictions to be made about the future. Sometimes, the fact that the claimant is entitled to a substantial award of damages will have an important bearing on how the claimant will be assumed to act in the future, which in turn can affect the quantum of damages that need to be awarded in order to comply with the compensation principle. An issue arises here as to whether the claimant's claim should be valued before any discount is made to the claimant's damages on account of the contributory negligence doctrine or whether the reverse should occur. It has been held that the claimant's claim must be valued first. In *Sowden v Lodge*,[45] the claimant, who had suffered personal injuries, was held 50% responsible for the damage on account of her contributory negligence. It was contended that, because of the large discount, the claimant would be unlikely to be able to afford to be cared for privately for the rest of her life, and that it followed that it would be more appropriate for the claimant to be cared for in a cheaper, public facility and lower damages awarded accordingly. This argument was rejected on the basis that the claim had to be valued first and any reduction in damages for contributory negligence applied only once the recoverable damages had been determined. Pill LJ said that '[d]amages are to be reduced having regard only to the 'claimant's share in the responsibility for the damage'. That assumes an assessment of the sum recoverable prior to any reduction for contributory negligence.'[46] **4.16**

[45] [2004] EWCA Civ 1370, [2005] 1 WLR 2129.
[46] ibid [79].

5

PROCEDURE

Statement of value on claim form. A claimant, in commencing a claim for money, must state on the claim form how much he or she expects to recover.[1] When estimating the sum that the claimant expects to recover, the effect of the contributory negligence doctrine should be disregarded.[2] 5.01

Track allocation. The courts are not required to accept the value that the claimant places on his or her case for the purposes of determining the track to which the case should be allocated. Where the court considers that the claimant has placed too high a value on the claim, the court can determine its estimated value. However, in exercising this power, the question of contributory negligence will not be taken into account.[3] 5.02

The burden of pleading. The defendant must specifically plead contributory negligence. In *UCB Bank Plc v David J Pinder Plc*, HHJ Hicks QC said that the 'authorities establish the necessity of pleading contributory negligence before it can be considered'.[4] The judge went on to hold that, once pleaded, the court is required to consider the doctrine even though the defendant declines to participate further in the proceedings and does not appear at the trial. However, in *Taylor v Simon Carves Ltd*,[5] it was held that where the plea of contributory negligence had not been pursued, it would be inappropriate for it to be considered further. 5.03

The burden of proof and its discharge. The defendant carries the onus of proving that the claimant was guilty of contributory negligence.[6] Proof to the civil standard is required to discharge that onus. Establishing that it is a 'strong possibility' that the claimant is guilty of contributory negligence is not enough.[7] The 5.04

---

1 CPR 16.3(2)(a).

2 CPR 16.3(6)(b).

3 CPR 26.8(2)(d).

4 [1998] CLC 1262 (QBD) [17]. See also *Fookes v Slayton* [1978] 1 WLR 1293 (CA).

5 1958 SLT (Sh Ct) 23 (Lothian and Borders Sheriff Court) 23 (William Garrett QC).

6 *Wakelin v London & South Western Railway Co* (1886) 12 App Cas 41 (HL) 47 (Lord Watson) ('I am of opinion that the onus of proving affirmatively that there was contributory negligence on the part of the person injured rests, in the first instance, upon the defendants, and that in the absence of evidence tending to that conclusion, the plaintiff is not bound to prove the negative in order to entitle her to a verdict in her favour').

7 *Dawes v Aldis* [2007] EWHC 1831 (QB) [33] (Eady J).

defendant does not need to lead any evidence in order to discharge its burden. Contributory negligence can be established on the basis of evidence adduced by the claimant.[8]

5.05 **When the issue of contributory negligence falls to be considered.** A judge called on to decide whether the contributory negligence doctrine applies should turn attention to it only once he or she has determined that the defendant breached an obligation owed to the claimant.[9]

5.06 **Summary judgment.** A defendant cannot avoid having summary judgment being entered simply by alleging contributory negligence, especially where the facts on which the defendant relies are insufficient to justify finding contributory negligence.[10]

5.07 **Issue estoppel.** The mere fact that liability has been determined against a defendant, whether on the basis of summary judgment, default judgment, or judgment following a trial, does not prevent the defendant from arguing the contributory negligence doctrine. The doctrine can be raised for the first time on the assessment of damages provided that 'the judgment [has] not settled any issue on which an allegation of contributory negligence would depend'.[11]

5.08 **The damages pre-discount and post-discount must be ascertained.** The apportionment legislation provides that when contributory negligence is established and the question of apportionment arises, the total damages to which the claimant would have been entitled had there been no contributory negligence and the extent to which the damages are to be discounted on account of the claimant's fault must be specified.[12] The purpose of this requirement is evidently to ensure that if the finding of contributory negligence or the apportionment of responsibility is disturbed on appeal a retrial will not necessarily be required to establish the quantum of the claim.

5.09 **Courts of limited jurisdiction.** Where proceedings are issued in a court of limited jurisdiction but the quantum of the claim, before any discount is made for contributory negligence, exceeds the court's jurisdiction, the jurisdictional cap applies first and any discount to the claimant's damages to be made second.[13] For example, if the claim is worth £10,000 and the jurisdictional limit is £5,000, the claimant will be entitled to recover only £2,500 if he or she is guilty of contributory negligence in the order of 50%.

[8] *Morrison v Gardiner* [2005] CSOH 156 [7] (Lord Glennie).

[9] *Griffiths v Vauxhall Motors Ltd* [2003] EWCA Civ 412 [24] (Clarke LJ).

[10] *Barnes v Nayer* The Times, 1 December 1986 (CA).

[11] *Maes Finance Ltd v AL Phillips & Co (a firm)* The Times, 25 March 1997 (Ch D) (Sir Richard Scott VC). See also *Pankhurst v White* [2006] EWHC 2093 (QB) [1] (Wilkie J); *Lunnun v Singh* The Times, 19 July 1999 (CA).

[12] Law Reform (Contributory Negligence) Act 1945, s 1(2) and (6); Law Reform (Miscellaneous Provisions) (Northern Ireland) Act 1948, s 2(1) and (6).

[13] *Kelly v Stockport Corpn* [1949] 1 All ER 893 (CA). See also *Sowden v Lodge* [2004] EWCA Civ 1370, [2005] 1 WLR 2129 (CA).

Interim payments. A court cannot order an interim payment to be made that exceeds a reasonable proportion of the likely amount of the final award.[14] The purpose of this restriction is to safeguard the defendant from the risk of being made to pay an amount greater than that for which he or she is liable. Consistently with this concern, the court is required when making such an order to take account of any discount that would likely be made by reason of the claimant's contributory negligence.[15] 5.10

Costs generally. Where a claimant establishes a right to a remedy but the damages are discounted for contributory negligence, the claimant will generally be entitled to a costs order in his or her favour.[16] In *Onay v Brown*, Goldring LJ held that, in a case in which the parties had agreed to a 25% discount, 'it [would be] wholly artificial to describe the claimant as other than the winner'.[17] In *Sonmez v Kebabery Wholesale Ltd*, the claimant did not concede that he was guilty of contributory negligence and that question was tried as a preliminary issue. It was found that the claimant was guilty of contributory negligence in the order of 20%. *Onay* was followed and it was held that the claimant was entitled to his costs in connection with the preliminary issue.[18] There is no rule that such a claimant is entitled to recover costs only in proportion to the defendant's share of responsibility for the damage.[19] 5.11

Costs: failed or abandoned allegations of contributory negligence by victorious defendant. Where a defendant fails on or abandons some but not all allegations of contributory negligence, such failure or abandonment may be taken into account in the court's orders regarding costs pursuant to the jurisdiction to award costs based on the extent to which the parties succeeded on various issues,[20] and in light of the reasonableness of raising particular allegations.[21] However, the courts will generally analyse the invocation of the contributory negligence doctrine holistically and will not deprive a victorious defendant of an order in respect of the costs incurred simply because certain allegations of contributory negligence were withdrawn or were unsuccessful. In *Governors and Company of the Bank of Ireland v Watts Group Plc*, Coulson J said:[22] 5.12

> [Counsel for the claimant] argued that, because [the defendant] abandoned a number of contributory negligence allegations at the start of trial, the [claimant] should have the costs of those abandoned allegations. I do not accept that submission. I consider that it is important for the court to look at the costs in the round.

---

14 CPR 25.7(4).

15 CPR 25.7(5)(a).

16 CPR 44.2(2)(a) ('If the court decides to make an order about costs—(a) the general rule is that the unsuccessful party will be ordered to pay the costs of the successful party …').

17 [2009] EWCA Civ 775, [2010] 1 Costs LR 29 [29].

18 [2009] EWCA Civ 1386 [22] (Ward LJ).

19 *'KRYSIA' Maritime Inc v Intership Ltd* [2008] EWHC 1880 (Admlty), [2009] 1 All ER (Comm) 292 [29] (Aikens J).

20 CPR 44.2(4)(b).

21 CPR 44.2(5)(b).

22 [2017] EWHC 2472 (TCC), [2017] 5 Costs LR 899 [12].

The contributory negligence case was successful. The fact that some of the individual allegations of contributory negligence were deleted at the start of the trial is, in my view, simply part of the rough and tumble of the trial process. It is not a matter that should be marked by an adverse order as to costs.

5.13 **Costs: fast track.** The maximum trial costs in cases that have been allocated to the fast track are capped by reference to the value of the claim.[23] For the purposes of valuing the claim, any discount for contributory negligence is disregarded.[24]

5.14 **Recoupment.** Legislation[25] provides for recoupment of certain state benefits from damages awards.[26] The statutory system makes no allowance for the recoupment to be reduced on account of the claimant's damages having been discounted for contributory negligence. Accordingly, two claimants who are identically positioned in terms of the quantum of their claim and benefits received, save that one is guilty of major contributory negligence and the other is not guilty of contributory negligence at all, will be liable to have same sums recouped from their compensation. A different regime applies in relation to certain NHS charges in respect of incidents occurring on or after 29 January 2007, where the recovery of prescribed NHS charges will be diminished in line with the extent to which, if at all, the claimant's compensation has been discounted for contributory negligence.[27]

---

[23] CPR 45.38.

[24] CPR 45.38(3)(a)(ii).

[25] Social Security (Recovery of Benefits) Act 1997.

[26] For discussion, see Peter Cane and James Goudkamp, *Atiyah's Accidents, Compensation and the Law* (9th edn, CUP 2018) 360–65.

[27] Health and Social Care (Community Health Standards) Act 2003, Pt 3.

6

APPEALS

(1) Applicable Law

Permission to appeal. In the case of England and Wales, permission is needed to appeal to the Court of Appeal from a decision of a county court or of the High Court.[1] Permission will be given only where the court from which permission is sought considers that the appeal would have a 'real prospect of success' or 'there is some other compelling reason for the appeal to be heard'.[2] An appeal will have 'a real prospect of success' when the prospect is realistic as opposed to fanciful.[3] In relation to Scotland, a litigant can appeal against the decision of a sheriff to the Sheriff Appeal Court without permission.[4] However, appeals lie from the Sheriff Appeal Court to the Court of Session only with permission.[5] Permission may be granted only where the appeal would 'raise an important point of principle or practice' or 'there is some other compelling reason for the Court of Session to hear the appeal'.[6] Permission is not required to appeal to the Court of Appeal in Northern Ireland save in relation to issues that are presently irrelevant.[7] 6.01

The circumstances in which appellate interference is permissible. In *Jackson v Murray*, Lord Reed said that an appeal should be allowed only where there is 'an identifiable error, such as an error of law, or the taking into account of an irrelevant matter, or the failure to take account of a relevant matter' or where the trial court's conclusion 'was not one which was reasonably open to it'.[8] Lord Reed made these remarks with regard to appeals relating to the apportionment of responsibility. Appeals regarding the existence of contributory negligence will generally attack findings of fact, and it is well established that appeals regarding findings of fact are governed by essentially the same test as that set out in *Jackson*.[9] 6.02

1 CPR 52.3.
2 CPR 52.6(1).
3 *Tanfern Ltd v Cameron-MacDonald* [2000] 1 WLR 1311 (CA) [21] (Brooke LJ).
4 Courts Reform (Scotland) Act 2014, s 110.
5 ibid s 113(1).
6 ibid s 113(2).
7 See Judicature (Northern Ireland) Act 1978, s 35.
8 [2015] UKSC 5, [2015] 2 All ER 805 [35].
9 See *Henderson v Foxworth Investments Ltd* [2014] UKSC 41, [2014] 1 WLR 2600 [67] (Lord Reed) ('in the absence of some other identifiable error, such as (without attempting an exhaustive

6.03 **Factual finding not reasonably open to the trial judge.** The circumstances in which a first instance judge will be found to have erred in the conclusion the judge reached on the facts depend on the extent of the advantage that the judge enjoyed by reason of having seen the witnesses. It is well established that '[t]he greater that advantage, the more reluctant the appellate court should be to interfere'.[10] Thus, if the trial judge reached his or her findings on issues relevant to the contributory negligence doctrine solely on the basis of written evidence, then appellate interference will be justified more readily than where the judge heard oral evidence.

6.04 **Errors in the apportionment of responsibility.** Because the apportionment of responsibility is a highly discretionary exercise,[11] an appeal in relation to any given apportionment will not be allowed 'merely on the basis of a disagreement as to the precise figure'[12] by which damages should be discounted. Rather, interference will be justified only 'in very exceptional circumstances'[13] and where the apportionment of responsibility fell beyond the 'acceptable range'.[14] The reasons for appellate restraint in this connection were explained by Kirby J in *Roads and Traffic Authority of New South Wales v Dederer* as follows:[15]

> This Court has said many times that appellate courts must show restraint in disturbing the apportionment ordered for contributory negligence as between a plaintiff and a defendant, having regard to their respective shares of responsibility for the damage. The point is self-evident. Involved in such an apportionment is a comparative examination of the whole conduct of each negligent party in relation to the circumstances of the accident and an evaluation of the comparative importance of the respective acts and omissions of the parties in causing the damage. Such decisions are evaluative and multi-factorial. Generally speaking, a trial judge, who has full knowledge of all of the evidence, will be in a better position to make such an apportionment correctly. An appellate court, even if it would have reached a different conclusion, will usually be hard pressed to identify an error that warrants disturbance of the primary judge's conclusion on such an issue. Tinkering with apportionments is to be discouraged.

The reticence of appellate courts to intervene as regards the apportionment of responsibility is such that appellate courts may decline to intervene even where the trial judge gave no reasons for his or her conclusions.[16]

---

account) a material error of law, or the making of a critical finding of fact which has no basis in the evidence, or a demonstrable misunderstanding of relevant evidence, or a demonstrable failure to consider relevant evidence, an appellate court will interfere with the findings of fact made by a trial judge only if it is satisfied that his decision cannot reasonably be explained or justified').

10 *Desir v Alcide* [2015] UKPC 24 [25] (Lord Clarke).

11 See 3.13.

12 *Jackson v Murray* [2015] UKSC 5, [2015] 2 All ER 805 [38] (Lord Reed).

13 *British Fame (Owners) v Macgregor (Owners) (The Macgregor)* [1943] AC 197 (HL) 201 (Lord Wright).

14 *Pride Valley Foods Ltd v Hall & Partners* 2001 WL 676719 (CA) [53] (Dyson LJ).

15 [2007] HCA 42, (2007) 234 CLR 330 [168] (footnote omitted).

16 See, eg, *Pride Valley Foods Ltd v Hall & Partners* 2001 WL 676719 (CA) [53] (Dyson LJ); cf *Starks v Chief Constable of Hertfordshire* [2013] EWCA Civ 782, [2014] RTR 4 [16] (Underhill LJ) ('I have less compunction in differing from [the trial judge's apportionment] because she did

Duty to allow an appeal where error exists. Despite the need for restraint in appeals in relation to contributory negligence, and particularly in relation to the apportionment of responsibility, where an error 'is clearly discernible' the appellate court 'must . . . interfere'.[17] In such circumstances, there is not merely a power to interfere but a duty to do so.[18] 6.05

Orders to be made where an appeal is allowed. If an appeal is allowed, the appellate court may remit the proceedings to the first instance judge. Alternatively, if the appellate court feels that it is able to dispose of the proceedings without further facts being found, it can make the necessary determinations itself.[19] 6.06

Where contributory negligence doctrine not considered by the courts below. It seems that an appellate court will generally not consider the issue of contributory negligence where it was not addressed by the court or courts below. These circumstances obtained in *Corr v IBC Vehicles Ltd* and a majority of the House of Lords considered that it would be inappropriate to deal with the question of contributory negligence as a result.[20] 6.07

Appeals to the Supreme Court. Permission to appeal to the Supreme Court will not be granted unless the case 'raise[s] an arguable point of law of general public importance'.[21] Accordingly, permission to appeal will rarely be given to challenge an apportionment of responsibility for contributory negligence.[22] However, where permission to appeal has been given, the Supreme Court will disturb an apportionment of responsibility in the same circumstances as will any other appellate court.[23] That approach, presumably, would also be taken in relation to an appeal regarding the existence of contributory negligence. 6.08

(2) Appellate Intervention in Practice

The incidence of appellate intervention. According to a study of 112 appellate decisions in England and Wales decided between 2000 and 2015 regarding the law of contributory negligence,[24] appeals as to the existence of contributory negligence were allowed in 42% of cases and as to the apportionment of responsibility in 34%. The composite rate of appellate intervention was 38%. The lower incidence of intervention in relation to the discount is consistent with the 6.09

not give any reason for her apportionment: she simply referred to the relevant legal principles and announced her conclusion').

17 *Smith v Chief Constable of Nottinghamshire Police* [2012] EWCA Civ 161, [2012] RTR 23 [36] (Ward LJ).

18 *Hicks v British Transport Commission* [1958] 1 WLR 493 (CA) 507 (Parker LJ).

19 See *Heaton v Herzog* [2008] EWCA Civ 1636, [2009] RTR 30 [15] (Sir William Aldous).

20 [2008] UKHL 13, [2008] 1 AC 884.

21 PD 3, r 3.3.3.

22 See *Jackson v Murray* [2015] UKSC 5, [2015] 2 All ER 805 [30] (Lord Reed).

23 ibid.

24 James Goudkamp and Donal Nolan, 'Contributory Negligence in the Court of Appeal: An Empirical Study' (2017) 37 Legal Studies 437.

principle that judges should be particularly reluctant to disturb determinations regarding the appropriate apportionment of responsibility.[25] Despite this, it is interesting to observe that there were more appeals in relation to the appropriate discount (56% of the total) than in relation to whether the claimant was guilty of contributory negligence (46%). Appeals were particularly unlikely to succeed in occupiers' liability cases (15%), with appellate judges being more willing to interfere in road accident (47%) and employers' liability (38%) cases.

6.10 **Who wins appeals?** Claimants brought 41% of the appeals in the study dataset and defendants 59%. 38% of the appeals in relation to the existence of contributory negligence were brought by claimants and 62% by defendants, whereas claimants brought 43% of the appeals concerning the size of the discount and defendants 57%. Claimants succeeded in 41% of appeals overall, with a success rate of 58% regarding the existence of contributory negligence and 30% in relation to the discount. By contrast, defendants won only 31% of their appeals overall, with the success rates in appeals with regards to the existence of contributory negligence (32%) and as to the discount (31%) being very similar. Hence, while the chances of a successful appeal on the apportionment of responsibility were similar for claimants and defendants, claimants were almost twice as likely to win appeals concerning the existence of contributory negligence as defendants.

6.11 **Adjustments in the size of the discount on appeal.** When an appeal was allowed in relation to the size of the discount, which occurred in 19 of the 112 cases studied, the discount was reduced in eight of these cases and increased in the other 11. The average reduction in the discount (31%) was considerably larger than the average increase in the discount (20%). Similarly, both the smallest reduction (20%) and the largest reduction (50%) were greater than the equivalent figures for increases in the discount (8.3% and 30%, respectively). Hence, it seems that when appellate courts reduce the discount, they tend to do so by larger amounts than when they increase the discount. The discount was rarely changed in either direction by a small amount. In only one claim was the change in the discount less than 10%, and in only four claims was it less than 20%. These results are consistent with the principle that appellate interference on discount is justified only where the appellate court concludes that the first instance court's decision was manifestly wrong.[26]

6.12 **Children.** In the study of appellate decisions on contributory negligence, children brought 12% of the claims where it was possible to tell whether a human claimant was an adult or child. The youngest claimants were aged 13. The rate of appellate interference in relation to the discount was much higher where the claimant was a child (78%) than an adult (28%). However, when the discount was disturbed, there was a marginal preference for increasing it in cases involving both child claimants (57%) and adult claimants (55%). It thus appears that although appellate courts are more likely to differ from a first instance court on the

[25] See 6.04.
[26] See 6.04.

appropriate discount where the claimant is a child, this does not translate into any clear tendency to lean either in favour of or against child claimants on the apportionment question. There were too few child cases involving appeals as to the existence of contributory negligence for meaningful conclusions to be drawn therefrom.

Part III

7

FREQUENTLY RECURRING SITUATIONS: INTRODUCTION

Part III explores the discounts imposed for contributory negligence in frequently recurring situations. In this chapter, the methodology employed is explained and details regarding the techniques used to describe the data are given. **7.01**

(1) Methodology

Temporal scope. Part III is concerned with the period 1 January 1998 to 31 December 2017: a twenty-year period. Part III thus concentrates on the contemporary operation of the law of contributory negligence. It is likely that the way in which judges reduce damages for contributory negligence has varied over time, given that major societal and economic changes have taken place since the apportionment legislation was enacted (such as the introduction of laws making the use of seat belts mandatory).[1] By looking only to cases decided since 1998, there is a reduced risk that different approaches that may have prevailed in earlier times will undermine attempts to understand how judges discount damages for contributory negligence in the present day. **7.02**

Claims rather than cases. The concern is with claims rather than with cases. A case is a single proceeding before a court. By contrast, a claim is a dispute between one claimant and one defendant. It is commonplace for a case to involve more than one claim, such as when two claimants sue a single defendant in the same proceedings. Where a case involves more than one claim and the claimant (or claimants) is guilty of contributory negligence, the court may reduce damages by different amounts in each claim. For example, if C1 and C2 sue D, the discount for contributory negligence in the claim by C1 may be 30%, whereas the discount in the claim by C2 may be 50%. In order to capture such differences, the analysis that follows concentrates on claims rather than cases. This approach means that a given case often features more than once in a particular sample of claims. **7.03**

Identification of claims. The claims on which the analysis in Part III is based were identified from searches of the major databases (Westlaw, LexisNexis, and Lawtel). **7.04**

[1] But see 3.29.

Our search terms, which were entered in the full text dialogue box, were 'Law Reform (Contributory Negligence) Act 1945' and 'contributory negligence'. All of the search results were reviewed and claims were included in the dataset where the court considered how to apportion responsibility for the claimant's damage following a finding of contributory negligence.

7.05 **Excluded claims.** Certain types of claim have been excluded from the analysis. By far the most important type of claim to be excluded are claims where the court made a merely contingent determination regarding the appropriate discount for contributory negligence. It is routine for trial judges who enter a verdict for the defendant in a given case, or who hold that the claimant was not guilty of contributory negligence, to nevertheless consider the issue of apportionment and to reach hypothetical findings in this connection, although the practice in this regard is not uniform.[2] Trial judges generally proceed in this way in case their decision on liability or their finding that the claimant was not guilty of contributory negligence is reversed on appeal. Where this occurs, the previously contingent finding regarding contributory negligence will morph into a finding that has substantive effect, and the need for a retrial on the issue of contributory negligence will thereby be avoided.[3] Claims involving contingent determinations have been excluded from our analysis because trial judges who consider the issue of contributory negligence contingently sometimes treat that issue somewhat cursorily, and so we took the view that these claims were less valuable as a guide to judicial decision-making on the apportionment issue. Other disregarded types of claim include professional negligence claims in which the existence of contributory negligence was in issue only in the underlying proceedings;[4] claims in which the issue was whether the doctrine of contributory negligence applied to the cause of action in question, and not how the doctrine, if it did apply, affected the outcome of the case on the facts;[5] and claims in which foreign law was applied on the issue of contributory negligence.[6]

7.06 **Appeals.** The chapters in this part of the book are concerned only with the discount that was ultimately imposed in the proceedings. Thus, where an appellate court interfered with a discount for contributory negligence that was made at first instance, only data from the appellate decision were included in the analysis, although we sometimes mention the finding at first instance and note that it was

[2] For illustrations of cases in which judges refused to address the question of contributory negligence or apportionment of responsibility on a hypothetical basis on the basis that the findings that they had made rendered doing so inappropriate, see *Norman v Theodore Goddard* [1992] BCC 14 (Ch D) 27 (Hoffmann J); *Gorham v British Telecommunications Plc* [2000] 1 WLR 2129 (CA) 2144 (Pill LJ); *Webster v Ridgeway Foundation School* [2010] EWHC 157 (QB) [196] (Nicol J); *Probert v Moore* [2012] EWHC 2324 (QB) [49] (David Pittaway QC); *Seery v Leathes Prior (a firm)* [2017] EWHC 80 (QB) [68] (Sir David Eady).

[3] Consider Lady Paton's exhortation to trial judges in *Little v Glen* [2014] CSIH 99 [35].

[4] See, eg, *Hunter v Earnshaw* [2001] PNLR 42 (QBD).

[5] See, eg, *Standard Chartered Bank v Pakistan National Shipping Corp (Nos 2 and 4)* [2003] UKHL 43, [2003] 1 AC 959.

[6] See, eg, *Barings Plc (in liq) v Coopers & Lybrand (No 7)* [2003] EWHC 1319 (Ch), [2003] PNLR 34; *Vann v Ocidental-Companhia De Seguros SA* [2015] EWCA Civ 572.

overturned. Where an appellate court set aside a finding of contributory negligence, the apportionment decision at first instance was disregarded.

Complex cases involving multiple acts of contributory negligence. Where the facts of a given claim fell within a particular category of recurrent act, the claim concerned was included within that category even if it was a 'complex' case in that it involved more than one act of contributory negligence. **7.07**

(2) Techniques Used to Describe the Data

Part III reports data that have been gathered from judicial decisions regarding the contributory negligence doctrine. Some of the techniques that are employed to describe these data will be familiar to readers, whereas others may be alien. It is necessary to explain those concepts with which not all readers may be acquainted along with some less-well-known aspects of otherwise familiar concepts. **7.08**

The average. The average is an everyday way of conveying meaning in relation to data. However, several features of that concept merit some brief remarks. The average is a measure of central tendency, that is to say, it is an attempt to identify the typical value in a given sample. It is calculated by dividing all values by the number of values. As a concept, the idea of the average is easy to grasp and it often conveys a significant amount of information. However, an average should be interpreted cautiously when the amount of data from which it has been calculated is limited. That is because, in such circumstances, the average is more prone to being distorted by outliers (ie atypical data) than would otherwise be the case. When a given sample that is treated in this volume contains outliers, the average is reported both with and without the outlier included in the calculations in order that the effect of the outlier on the average can be seen by the reader. **7.09**

The mode. The mode is another frequently used measure of central tendency. It refers to the value that appears most commonly in a given sample. Suppose that the following discounts for contributory negligence are imposed: 10, 10, 20, 20, 20, 40, 45, 60, 75, 75, 80, and 80. In this instance, the mode would be 20. Unlike the average, the mode is not influenced by outliers. However, the mode, in contrast with the average, ignores all of the data save for the most frequently occurring value. The mode will sometimes be the same as (or close to) the average but this will not necessarily be the case. A given sample may have more than one mode and, if no values recur, no mode at all. **7.10**

The standard deviation. The standard deviation is a measure of the variability of data. In other words, it reveals whether the data concerned are homogeneous or, conversely, heterogeneous. More specifically, the standard deviation is the average amount by which data diverge from the average. Suppose, for example, that the standard deviation for a given sample of discounts imposed for contributory negligence is 25%. That would mean that, on average, the discount imposed in each claim within the sample is 25% higher or lower than the average discount. A standard deviation of 25% is relatively large in **7.11**

the context of discounts for contributory negligence. It suggests that the data are reasonably dispersed from each other, on average. Conversely, a standard deviation of, say, 10% would mean that, on average, most data points are clustered within a reasonably confined bracket.

7.12 **The range.** The range refers to the difference between the highest and lowest value within a given sample. For example, if the highest discount for contributory negligence in a sample of claims is 80% and the lowest is 20%, the range would be 60%. Like the standard deviation, the range is a widely used measure of the variability of data. However, it is generally much less meaningful than the standard deviation because, unlike the standard deviation, it ignores most of the data. The range concentrates only on the most extreme values in the sample.

7.13 **Boxplots.** Boxplots that show the distribution of discounts for recurrent acts of contributory negligence are provided. An example of a boxplot can be seen in Figure 7.1. The thick black line in the boxplot represents the median discount value,[7] the box gives the first and third quartiles of the discount values, and the dotted lines extend out to 1.5 times the interquartile range (the range between the value at the first quartile and the third quartile). Outliers are drawn as dots.

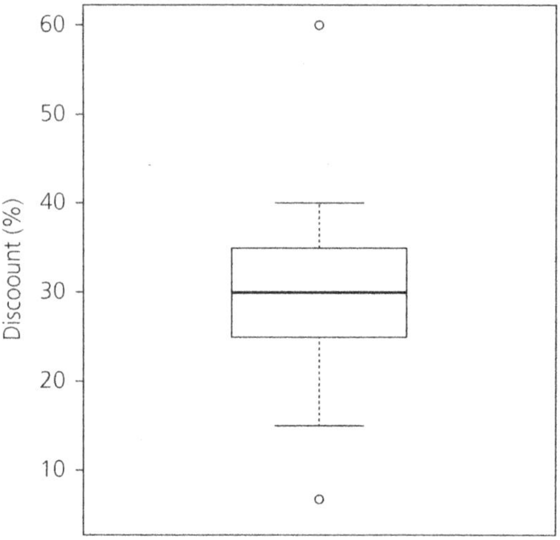

Figure 7.1 Illustration of a boxplot

[7] When there are an even number of claims, the median is the average of the centremost values.

8

INTOXICATED PEDESTRIAN INJURED BY MOTORIST

(1) Scope of this Chapter

This chapter concerns reductions in the damages that intoxicated pedestrians recovered from negligent motorists. 8.01

(2) Descriptive Statistics

Number of claims	14
Average discount	39.6%
Mode	30% and 33.3%
Highest discount	85%
Lowest discount	20%
Standard deviation	17.4%

Figure 8.1

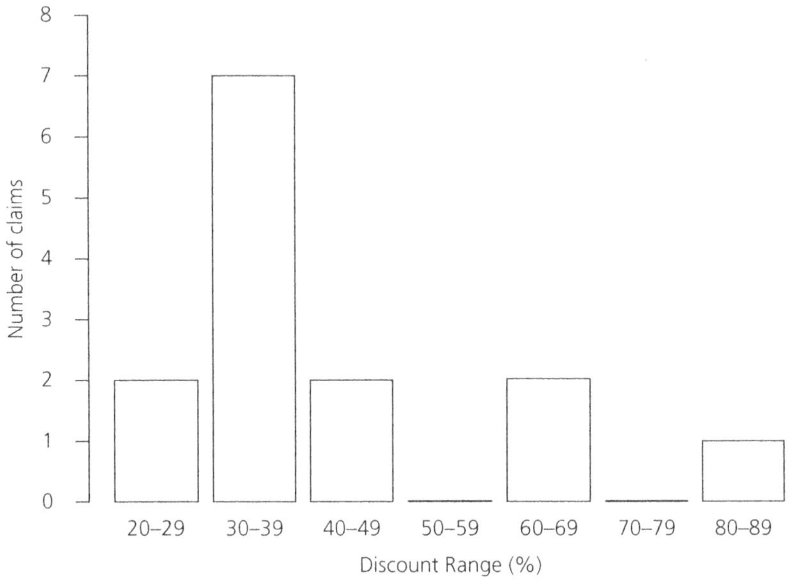

Figure 8.2 Number of claims by discount range

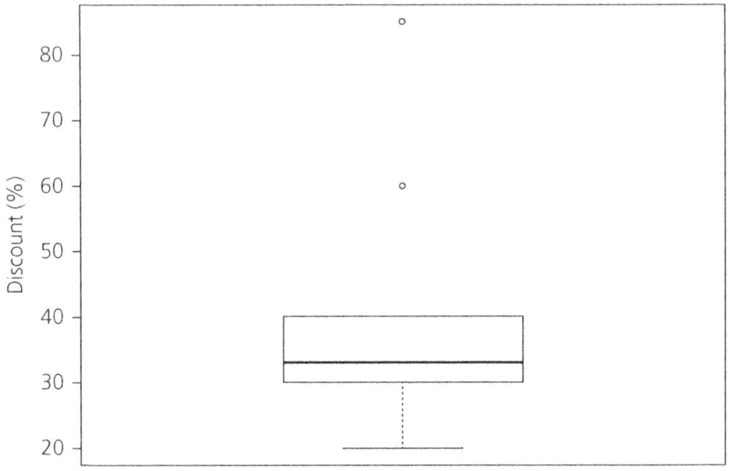

Figure 8.3 Boxplot of discounts

(3) Remarks Regarding the Statistics

8.02 The discounts imposed exhibit relatively little variability. Nearly all of the discounts fell between 20% and 40%. Two discounts of 60% and one discount of 85% are abnormal. There were no discounts below 20%, which suggests that that is the minimum discount that an intoxicated pedestrian who is guilty of contributory negligence can realistically expect in a claim against a negligent motorist.

8.03 The average discount of 39.6% is in line with the average discount of 40% that was observed in first instance claims generally.[1] It might be thought that the claim involving a discount of 85% exerts a significant influence on the average discount. However, this is not so, as the average discount falls only to 36.1% if that claim is excluded from consideration.

(4) Illustration of Case Involving a Discount Near the Average

8.04 In *Lightfoot v Go-Ahead Group Plc*,[2] the claimant, then aged 52, was struck by the defendant's bus. The accident happened at night-time on an unlit rural road. The bus was travelling at between 23 and 25 mph at the time of impact, with the applicable speed limit for buses being 50 mph. The claimant was 'very drunk'. He had proceeded diagonally into the carriageway and attempted to flag down the bus. The bus driver had been reading a laminated timetable with the cabin light activated at the time of the accident. Further, he was driving with dipped headlights. A 40% discount was imposed.

(5) Illustration of Case Involving a High Discount

8.05 In *Smith v Bluebird Buses Ltd*,[3] the pursuer, who was intoxicated, entered the carriageway in order to argue with a passenger in a vehicle that had stopped at the traffic lights. The pursuer turned away from that vehicle and walked a few steps without looking for oncoming traffic. At that point, the pursuer was struck by the defender's bus. The bus had been travelling at between 5 and 10 mph at the time. The court found that '[t]he driver had little opportunity to avoid the collision', although his view of the pursuer was unobstructed. An 85% discount was imposed.

(6) Illustration of Case Involving a Low Discount

8.06 The accident in *Ayres v Odedra*[4] occurred just after midnight on a one-way street within a pedestrianized zone in the centre of a city and close to a pedestrian crossing. The claimant, then aged 24, was drunk and unsteady on his feet. He placed himself in front of the defendant's vehicle, which had stopped at traffic lights. The claimant then dropped his trousers and remained on the road after

[1] See 3.24.
[2] [2011] EWHC 89 (QB), [2001] RTR 27.
[3] [2014] CSOH 75, 2014 Rep LR 91.
[4] [2013] EWHC 40 (QB).

the traffic lights had turned green. The claimant was struck when the defendant proceeded to drive forward. A 20% discount was imposed.

(7) Claims in the Sample for this Chapter

8.07 (1) *Ayres v Odedra* [2013] EWHC 40 (QB) (20%); (2) *Sedge v Prime* [2011] EWHC 820 (QB) (25%); (3) *Cook v Thorne* [2001] EWCA Civ 81 (30%); (4) *Cook v Thorne* [2001] EWCA Civ 81 (30%); (5) *Wooldridge v George* (QBD, 23 January 2017) (30%); (6) *Griffiths v Brown* [1999] PIQR P131 (QBD) (33.3%); (7) *Lunt v Khelifa* 2000 WL 1479700 (QBD) (33.3%); (8) *Smith v Chief Constable of Nottinghamshire Police* [2012] EWCA Civ 161, [2012] RTR 23 (33.3%); (9) *Parkinson v Chief Constable of Dyfed Powys* [2004] EWCA Civ 802 (35%); (10) *Lightfoot v Go-Ahead Group Plc* [2011] EWHC 89 (QB), [2011] RTR 27 (40%); (11) *Eagle v Chambers (No 1)* [2003] EWCA Civ 1107, [2004] RTR 9 (40%); (12) *Green v Bannister* [2003] EWCA Civ 1819 (60%); (13) *McCaughey v Mullan* [2014] NIQB 132 (60%); (14) *Smith v Bluebird Buses Ltd* [2014] CSOH 75, 2014 Rep LR 91 (85%).[5]

[5] As to why the same case appears more than once in this sample, see 7.03.

9

NON-INTOXICATED PEDESTRIAN INJURED BY MOTORIST: ADULT PEDESTRIAN

(1) Scope of this Chapter

This chapter is concerned with adult pedestrians who were not intoxicated at the time and who were injured after moving into the path of oncoming traffic. **9.01**

(2) Descriptive Statistics

Number of claims	27
Average discount	40.9%
Mode	50%
Highest discount	80%
Lowest discount	10%
Standard deviation	20.1%

Figure 9.1

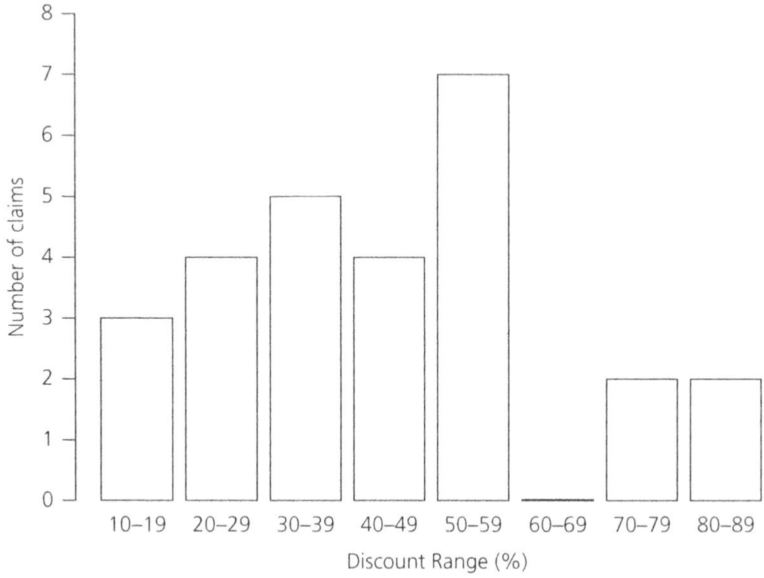

Figure 9.2 Number of claims by discount range

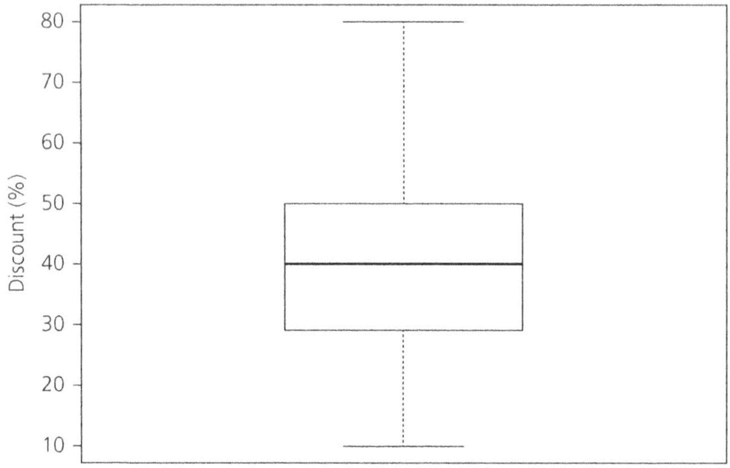

Figure 9.3 Boxplot of discounts

(3) Remarks Regarding the Statistics

9.02 The majority of the discounts were concentrated between 30% and 50%, although a substantial proportion fell towards the ends of the spectrum yielding a distribution that approximates a tri-modal one. It is striking that the average discount in the case of *non*-intoxicated adult pedestrians who were injured by a motorist (40.9%) is slightly *higher* than the average discount in claims by intoxicated pedestrians (39.6%).[1] The reason for this result is not immediately clear, although it does not appear to be due to the impact of outliers. One possible explanation lies in the idea that motorists are expected to take particular care when driving in areas where it is known that intoxicated pedestrians are likely to be present.

(4) Illustration of Case Involving a Discount Near the Average

In *McDonald v Chambers*,[2] the pursuer stepped from a traffic island into a road before establishing that there were no oncoming vehicles, although she had pushed the control button to bring up the walk signal. The defender motorist had seen the pursuer and had also noticed that she had pushed the control button. However, the defender drove through an amber light and struck the pursuer. Lord McCluskey said: 'A pedestrian who is using a set of traffic lights, with signals for both traffic and pedestrians, to cross a busy road can hardly escape a charge of carelessness if she steps into a roadway when the roadway is not clear or when there is traffic which is still moving towards the place where the pedestrians are to cross.'[3] Damages were reduced by 33.3%. **9.03**

(5) Illustration of Case Involving a High Discount

Watson v Skuse[4] involves an unusually high discount for a pedestrian case. The claimant was endeavouring to cross a road at a pelican crossing. He checked the traffic lights, which he noted were red, and started to cross the road. However, the claimant did not look at the pedestrian light, which was also red, and should have realized that the traffic lights were about to turn green. Upon entering the roadway, the claimant passed so closely in front of a large lorry with a sheer bonnet that its driver was unable to see him. When the traffic lights turned green, the lorry moved forward and struck the claimant. The claimant had been drinking but was not intoxicated. The trial judge held that the driver should have seen the claimant as he started to move into the road and ought to have anticipated that the claimant would act as he did. The Court of Appeal increased the discount of 50% that had been imposed at first instance to 80%. Sedley LJ described the claimant as being 'the principal author of his own misfortune' and added '[i]t was the claimant who [sought to cross the road] at a moment when he could and should have seen that the red pedestrian light was against him, so that the lights were about to change in **9.04**

[1] See 8.03.
[2] 2000 SLT 454 (OH).
[3] ibid 455.
[4] [2001] EWCA Civ 1158.

the defendant's favour'.[5] Arden LJ referred to the claimant as having taken 'a foolish gamble'.[6]

(6) Illustration of Case Involving a Low Discount

9.05 In *McDermott v Pettit*,[7] the claimant was struck by the defendant's car as he sought to cross a major arterial road in the early hours of the morning. The trial judge found that the defendant had a blood–alcohol content greater than the prescribed limit and had been driving significantly in excess of the speed limit. The claimant was found guilty of contributory negligence on the basis that he should have used a pedestrian crossing that was located just 10 m from where he had entered the road. The judge also emphasized that the road comprised a three-lane carriageway and that nearby traffic lights were showing green in favour of oncoming traffic. Several other pedestrians were milling around the area at the time of the accident. A 10% discount was imposed.

(7) Claims in the Sample for this Chapter

9.06 (1) *McDermott v Pettit* [2011] EWHC 3074 (QB) (10%); (2) *Sklair v Haycock* [2009] EWHC 3328 (QB) (10%); (3) *Douglas v O'Neill* [2011] EWHC 601 (QB) (12.5%); (4) *Bruma v Hassan* [2017] EWHC 3209 (QB) (20%); (5) *Carpenter v Lunnon* [2004] EWHC 3079 (QB) (20%); (6) *White v Chapman* 2001 WL 825325 (QBD) (20%); (7) *Sedge v Prime* [2011] EWHC 820 (QB) (25%); (8) *Belka v Prosperini* [2011] EWCA Civ 623 (33.3%); (9) *Greenwood v Cummings* (QBD, 9 April 2008) (33.3%); (10) *Markowski v Elson* [2001] CLY 4477 (Weymouth CC) (33.3%); (11) *McDonald v Chambers* 2000 SLT 454 (OH) (33.3%); (12) *Rooke v Liston* 1999 WL 477713 (CA) (33.3%); (13) *Brownlow v Knight* [2003] NIQB 71 (40%); (14) *George v Stagecoach South-East London* 2001 WL 513089 (QBD) (40%); (15) *Hickman v London Central Bus Company Ltd* [2013] EWHC 1703 (QB) (40%); (16) *Hughes-Jukes v Etti* [2006] EWHC 2493 (QB), [2007] RTR 2 (40%); (17) *Gonzalez-Ramirez v First Eastern Counties Buses Ltd* (QBD, 26 October 2017) (50%); (18) *Hill v Master Concrete Northern Ltd* [2010] EWHC 3613 (QB) (50%); (19) *McCreery v Letson* [2015] CSOH 153 (50%); (20) *Rehill v Rider Holdings Ltd* [2012] EWCA Civ 628, [2013] RTR 5 (50%); (21) *Rose v South East London and Kent Bus Company Ltd* [2004] EWHC 1106 (QB) (50%); (22) *Sahakian v McDonnell* [2007] EWHC 3242 (QB), [2008] RTR 19 (50%); (23) *Smeed v Sparrow* 1999 WL 477490 (CA) (50%); (24) *Bryce v McKirdy* 1999 SLT 988 (OH) (75%); (25) *Pritchard v Ralph* 2000 WL 1791426 (CA) (75%); (26) *Maughan v Boylan* [2006] NIQB 38 (80%); (27) *Watson v Skuse* [2001] EWCA Civ 1158 (80%).

---

[5] ibid [27].
[6] ibid [33].
[7] [2011] EWHC 3074 (QB).

10

NON-INTOXICATED PEDESTRIAN INJURED BY MOTORIST: CHILD PEDESTRIAN

(1) Scope of this Chapter

This chapter is concerned with child pedestrians who were injured after moving into the path of oncoming traffic and who were not intoxicated at the time. 10.01

(2) Descriptive Statistics

Number of claims	12
Average discount	39.8%
Mode	30%
Highest discount	75%
Lowest discount	15%
Standard deviation	20.9%

Figure 10.1

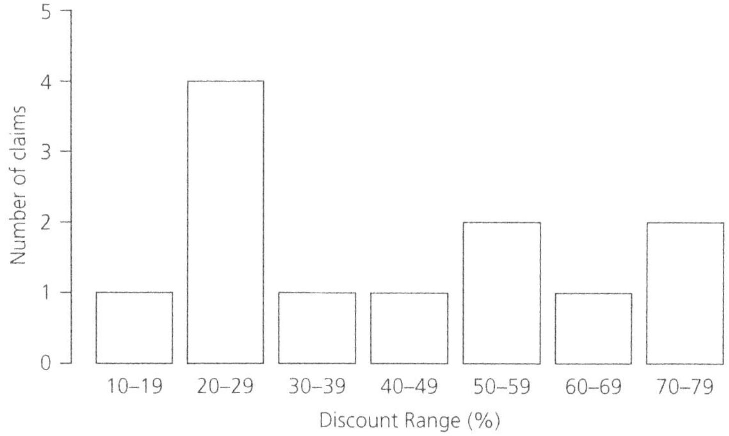

Figure 10.2 Number of claims by discount range

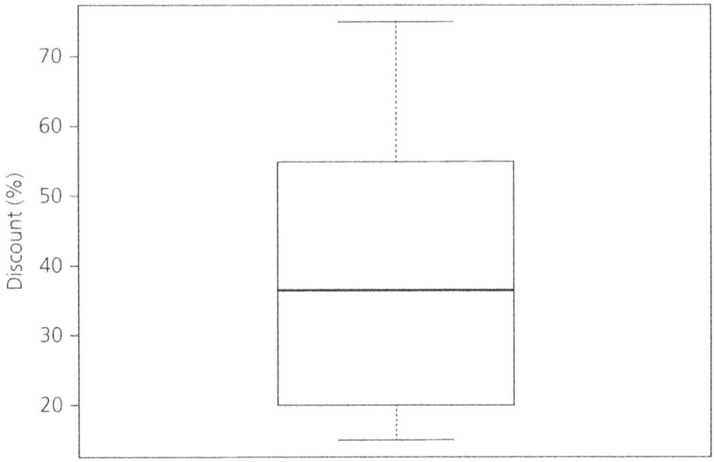

Figure 10.3 Boxplot of discounts

(3) Remarks Regarding the Statistics

10.02 A third of the claims on which this chapter is based involved discounts between 10% and 20%. The rest of the discounts were spread more or less evenly over most of the rest of the spectrum, with a small uptick in discounts between 30% and 50%.

10.03 The average discount in the claims on which this chapter is based (39.8%) is only a little below the average discount in the case of sober adult pedestrians who were injured by motorists (41.7%)[1] and is very close to the average discount in claims by intoxicated pedestrians (39.6%).[2] The relatively small number of claims on which the present chapter is based means that these results should be interpreted cautiously.

(4) Illustration of Case Involving a Discount Near the Average

10.04 *Eagle v Chambers*[3] is a well-known and important decision of the Court of Appeal. The claimant was aged 17 at the time of the accident, which occurred on a dual carriageway at night-time in good driving conditions. The claimant had entered and was walking along the roadway in a distressed state and had failed to heed at least two warnings that had been given to her by persons concerned for her safety.

[1] See 9.02.
[2] See 8.03.
[3] [2003] EWCA Civ 1107, [2004] RTR 9.

The defendant motorist, who had been driving at approximately 30 to 35 mph, collided with the claimant. An event had recently finished near the scene of the accident, and several pedestrians were walking on the footpath in the vicinity. The defendant had been drinking prior to the accident and admitted that he had drunk enough to impair his driving ability. He failed a roadside alcohol breath test but was found to be just below the limit when tested again at a police station. At first instance, damages were reduced by 60%. On appeal, the discount was reduced to 40%, with the Court of Appeal apparently finding that there was insufficient evidence to support the trial judge's conclusion that the claimant had been intoxicated.

(5) Illustration of Case Involving a High Discount

In *Paramasivan v Wicks*,[4] the claimant, then aged 13, was struck by the defendant's vehicle. The claimant had been standing outside a shop with several of his friends and had suddenly run into the road after throwing an ice cream at one of the group, apparently in order to avoid the consequences of doing so. The claimant passed between two parked cars. The defendant was found to have been driving too fast and to have been paying insufficient attention. The accident occurred at night-time. Hughes LJ said that the claimant was 'quite old enough to understand roads' and that it was he 'who created the hazard and he did it by doing something entirely unexpected and … very careless'.[5] Damages had been reduced by 50% at first instance. The discount was increased to 75% on appeal. **10.05**

(6) Illustration of Case Involving a Low Discount

In *AB v Main*,[6] the claimant suffered catastrophic brain injuries when, aged 8 years and 10 months, he was struck by the defendant's vehicle. The accident occurred in the afternoon. The road concerned had a single lane running in each direction and was a relatively busy one, with a speed limit of 40 mph. The claimant had been playing nearby and jogged into the road to fetch a bottle that was lying on the far side of it. The claimant was 'completely unaware' of the defendant's vehicle prior to its striking him. The trial judge found that the defendant had seen the claimant before he had entered the roadway, should have realized that the claimant was playing, should have reduced her speed, and should have moved into the centre of the road. The trial judge also found that the defendant had been driving at about 30 mph at the time of the impact. Damages were reduced by 20%. **10.06**

4 [2013] EWCA Civ 262.
5 ibid [17].
6 [2015] EWHC 3183 (QB).

(7) Claims in the Sample for this Chapter

10.07 (1) *SH v Farrell* [2007] NIQB 42 (15%); (2) *AB v Main* [2015] EWHC 3183 (QB) (20%); (3) *Honnor v Lewis* [2005] EWHC 747 (QB) (20%); (4) *McCluskey v Wallace* 1998 SLT 1357 (IH) (20%); (5) *Scutts v Keyse* 2000 WL 33201536 (QBD) (25%); (6) *Toropdar v D* [2009] EWHC 2997 (TCC) (33.3%); (7) *Eagle v Chambers* [2003] EWCA Civ 1107, [2004] RTR 9 (40%); (8) *Jackson v Murray* [2015] UKSC 5, [2015] 2 All ER 805 (50%); (9) *Rainford v Lawrenson* [2014] EWHC 1188 (QB) (50%); (10) *Futter v Bryceland* 2000 GWD 9-339 (OH) (60%); (11) *Ehrari v Curry* [2006] EWHC 1319 (QB) (70%); (12) *Paramasivan v Wicks* [2013] EWCA Civ 262 (75%).

11

FAILURE TO WEAR A SEAT BELT

(1) Scope of this Chapter

This chapter concerns claims that involve either a failure to wear a seat belt or a failure properly to use a seat belt. 11.01

(2) Descriptive Statistics

Number of claims	14
Average discount	21.6%
Mode	15%
Highest discount	50%
Lowest discount	10%
Standard deviation	10.9%

Figure 11.1

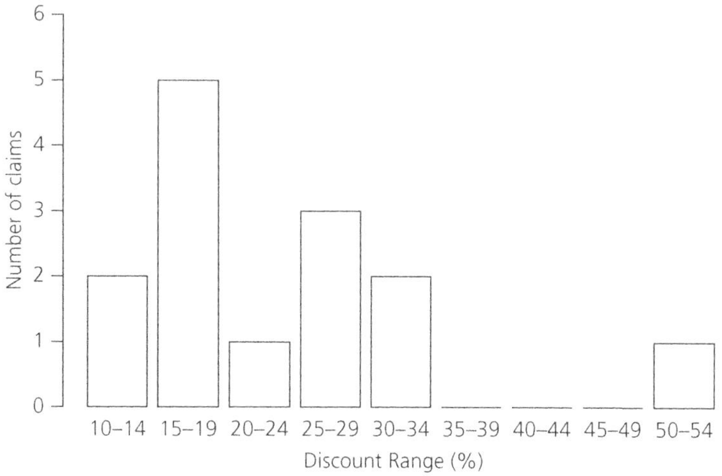

Figure 11.2 Number of claims by discount range

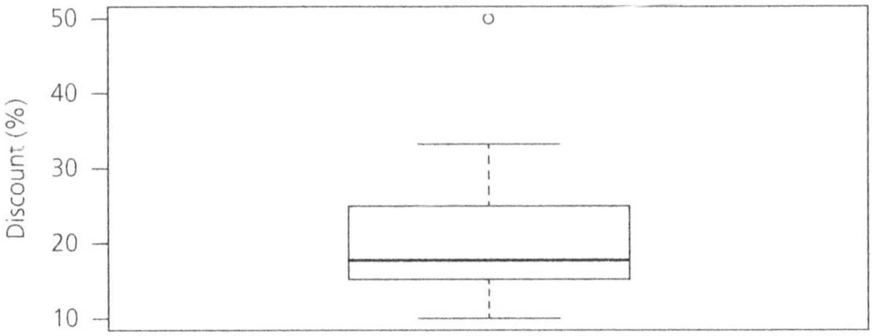

Figure 11.3 Boxplot of discounts

(3) Remarks Regarding the Statistics

11.02 The discounts imposed in the claims that are addressed in this chapter are relatively homogenous. Most of the discounts are clustered around the average discount (19.5%), with the range being just 23%. The concentration of claims within this narrow band is undoubtedly due to the guidelines that were established in *Froom v Butcher*[1] for apportionment in seat-belt cases. In *Froom*, Lord Denning MR, with whom the other members of the Court of Appeal agreed, held that, in the ordinary course of things, a discount of 25% for contributory negligence is appropriate if wearing a seat belt would have avoided the injury altogether, and a discount of 15% is appropriate where the injury would have been less serious had a seat belt been used. It is therefore unsurprising that the most common discount in this type of case was 15%.

11.03 The courts are relatively lenient in terms of the discounts imposed in this category of claim, with the average discount (19.5%) being less than half the average discount of 40% in first instance claims generally. This may in part be attributable to the fact that in virtually all (if not all) seat-belt cases the contributory negligence contributes only to the claimant's injuries and not to the accident that causes them.

(4) Illustration of Case Involving a Discount Near the Average

11.04 In *Hazlett v Robinson*,[2] the claimant suffered fractures of the leg, arm, and spine in an accident caused by the defendant's negligence. When the accident occurred, the claimant was sitting in the rear of a vehicle being driven by the defendant. The judge found that the claimant's injuries 'would have been very [much] less severe

[1] [1976] QB 286 (CA). See 3.28.
[2] [2014] NIQB 17.

had he been wearing a seatbelt'.[3] In reaching that conclusion, the judge accepted the evidence of two expert witnesses who had testified that fractures to the bones concerned were very unlikely to occur when a seat belt was used. A 20% discount was imposed.

(5) Illustration of Case Involving a High Discount

In *Eyres v Atkinsons Kitchens and Bedrooms Ltd*,[4] the claimant driver suffered severe spinal injuries when he fell asleep and his vehicle overturned. The claimant sued his employer alleging negligence in permitting him to drive when he was too tired to do so safely. At first instance a discount of 25% was imposed only on the basis that the claimant had not been wearing a seat belt. The Court of Appeal increased the discount to 33.3% on the ground that the claimant's contributory negligence had been aggravated by the fact that he drove while tired. Ward LJ remarked that the employer did 'nothing to guard against the very risk of injury from which he ought to have been saving his employee' and hence bore the bulk of the responsibility for the damage. A 33.3% discount was imposed. **11.05**

(6) Illustration of Case Involving a Low Discount

In *Mattar v Shenouda*,[5] the deceased, a 51-year-old man who had been sitting in the front passenger seat of the defendant's vehicle at the time of the accident, suffered fatal injuries due to the defendant's negligence. Buckley J held that had the deceased been wearing a seat belt he 'would not have been killed but would nevertheless have sustained multiple and fairly serious injury'. A 15% discount was imposed. **11.06**

(7) Claims in the Sample for this Chapter

(1) *Corbett v Cumbria Kart Racing Club* [2013] EWHC 1362 (QB) (10%); (2) *Corbett v Cumbria Kart Racing Club* [2013] EWHC 1362 (QB) (10%); (3) *Garth v Grant* (QBD, 25 May 2007) (15%); (4) *Edwards v Martin* [2010] EWHC 570 (QB) (15%); (5) *Mattar v Shenouda* 2001 WL 606384 (QBD) (15%); (6) *Palmer v Kitley* [2008] EWHC 2819 (QB) (15%); (7) *W v Hardman* [2001] CLY 4452 (Leeds CC) (15%); (8) *Hazlett v Robinson* [2014] NIQB 17 (20%); **11.07**

[3] ibid [53].
[4] [2007] EWCA Civ 365.
[5] 2001 WL 606384 (QBD).

(9) *Al Gouri v Achkar* [2007] CLY 3079 (QBD) (25%); (10) *Gawler v Raettig* [2007] EWHC 373 (QB) (25%); (11) *Pearson v Anwar* [2015] EWCA Civ 1011 (25%); (12) *Steele v WH Malcolm Ltd* 2013 GWD 25-511 (North Strathclyde Sheriff Court) (30%); (13) *Eyres v Atkinsons Kitchens & Bedrooms Ltd* [2007] EWCA Civ 365 (33.3%); (14) *Taylor v Leslie* 1998 SLT 1248 (OH) (50%).[6]

[6] As to why the same case appears more than once in this sample, see 7.03.

12

SPEEDING

(1) Scope of this Chapter

This chapter concerns claims made by motorists or motorcyclists who suffered injury while driving or riding too quickly. It includes cases in which the claimant, although travelling below the speed limit, was held to have been travelling too fast in all of the circumstances.[1] There was one claim in the study period brought by a bicyclist who was found to have been riding too quickly.[2] That claim has not been included in the analysis in this chapter. **12.01**

(2) Descriptive Statistics

Number of claims	20
Average discount	48.1%
Mode	50%
Highest discount	90%
Lowest discount	20%
Standard deviation	21.8%

Figure 12.1

[1] See, eg, *Edwards v Jerman* [2004] CLY 2743 (Liverpool CC) (25%); *Russell v West Sussex CC* [2009] EWHC 1063 (QB) (50%).

[2] *Brown v Brent* (Croydon CC, 21 June 2011) (33.3%).

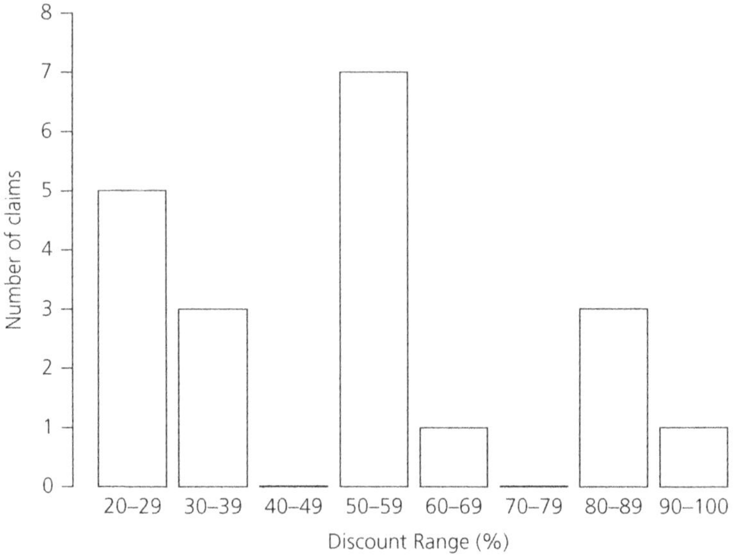

Figure 12.2 Number of claims by discount range

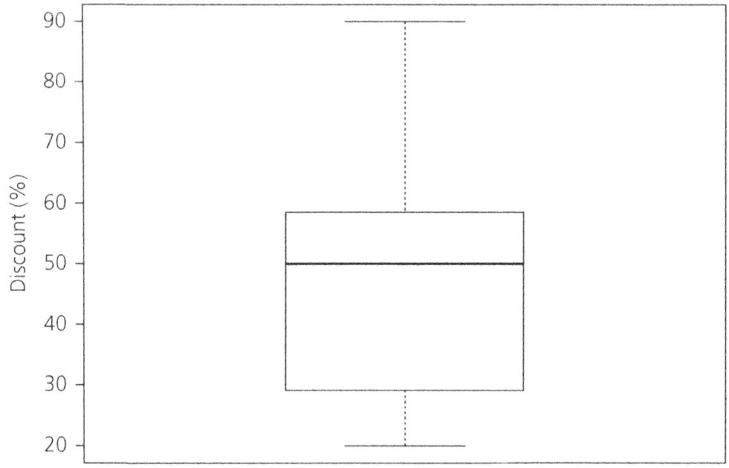

Figure 12.3 Boxplot of discounts

(3) Remarks Regarding the Statistics

12.02 The most notable feature of the statistics is the average discount of 48.1%, which is noticeably higher than the average discount of 40% across first instance decisions generally. It seems that the courts tend to regard speeding as conduct that involves greater culpability or causal potency than many other types of contributory negligence.[3]

(4) Illustration of Case Involving a Discount Near the Average

In *Russell v West Sussex CC*,[4] the claimant's vehicle skidded off the road and struck a tree. The claimant suffered severe injuries. The accident might not have happened if the road had been level with the verge. The verge was some 6 inches lower than the road at the point at which the vehicle left the road, and the drop resulted in the claimant needing to make a violent correction, which contributed to the vehicle slewing off the road. The speed limit was 60 mph and the claimant was found to have been driving at 45 mph at the time. However, the judge found that 45 mph was too fast given that it was a frosty morning and there was ice on the road. Damages were reduced by 50%. **12.03**

(5) Illustration of Case Involving a High Discount

In *Train v Secretary of State for Defence*,[5] the defendant, who was driving a minibus, turned in front of the deceased motorcyclist. The deceased braked but was unable to avoid the impact and was fatally injured. It was found that the defendant, who had seen the deceased, had negligently concluded that it was safe for him to turn across his path, having underestimated the speed at which the deceased was travelling. Although no precise finding was made as to the deceased's speed at the time of the accident, the judge said that he was travelling at 'a very high speed'[6] and 'probably in excess of 40mph',[7] even though the speed limit was 20 mph. An 80% discount was imposed. **12.04**

(6) Illustration of Case Involving a Low Discount

In *Day v Suffolk CC*,[8] the claimant suffered injury when his vehicle ran into a pothole on a rural, single-lane road near his home. The trial judge found that the claimant had been driving at about 25 mph. The claimant sued the highway authority that was responsible for maintaining the road, which owed him a duty under section 41 of the Highways Act 1980. The judge held that the claimant had **12.05**

[3] See 3.39.
[4] [2009] EWHC 1063 (QB).
[5] [2014] EWHC 1928 (QB), [2014] RTR 28.
[6] ibid [33].
[7] ibid [24].
[8] [2007] EWCA Civ 1436.

been driving too quickly given the road's condition, of which the claimant was aware, and in view of the need to keep a proper lookout for potholes. Damages were reduced by 25%, which discount the Court of Appeal with some reluctance declined to increase.

(7) Claims in the Sample for this Chapter

12.06 (1) *Ellis v Lokat* (QBD, 6 October 2011) (20%); (2) *Powell v Hansen* 2001 WL 753470 (QBD) (20%); (3) *Day v Suffolk CC* [2007] EWCA Civ 1436 (25%); (4) *Edwards v Jerman* [2004] CLY 2743 (Liverpool CC) (25%); (5) *Morrison v Gardiner* [2005] CSOH 156 (25%); (6) *Jones v Lawton* [2013] EWHC 4108 (QB) (33.3%); (7) *MacKenzie v Perth & Kinross Council* (OH, 22 January 2003) (33.3%); (8) *Nicolson v Willis* [2006] EWHC 2402 (QB) (33.3%); (9) *Buchan v Whiting* [2008] EWHC 2951 (QB) (50%); (10) *Gilfillan v Barbour* 2003 SLT 1127 (OH) (50%); (11) *Grace v Tanner* [2003] EWCA Civ 354 (50%); (12) *Jenkins v Holt* [1999] RTR 411 (CA) (50%); (13) *Russell v West Sussex CC* [2009] EWHC 1063 (QB) (50%); (14) *Woodham v M Turner (t/a Turners of Great Barton)* [2012] EWCA Civ 375 (50%); (15) *Wheeler v Chief Constable of Gloucestershire Constabulary* [2013] EWCA Civ 1791 (50%); (16) *Buswell v Symes* [2015] EWHC 1379 (QB) (66.6%); (17) *Burton v Evitt* [2011] EWCA Civ 1378 (80%); (18) *Ringe v Eden Springs (UK) Ltd* [2012] EWHC 14 (QB) (80%); (19) *Train v Secretary of State for Defence* [2014] EWHC 1928 (QB), [2014] RTR 28 (80%); (20) *Stephen v Peter* 2005 Rep LR 53 (OH) (90%).

13

SLIP-AND-FALL ACCIDENT: WORKPLACE

(1) Scope of this Chapter

This chapter concerns slip-and-fall accidents that occurred while the claimant was at work. It extends to all claims in which the claimant failed to pay attention to his or her footing or to dangers on the ground. It is not confined to situations where the claimant fell when on his or her employer's premises. **13.01**

(2) Descriptive Statistics

Number of claims	20
Average discount	37.3%
Mode	25% and 50%
Highest discount	75%
Lowest discount	15%
Standard deviation	16.7%

Figure 13.1

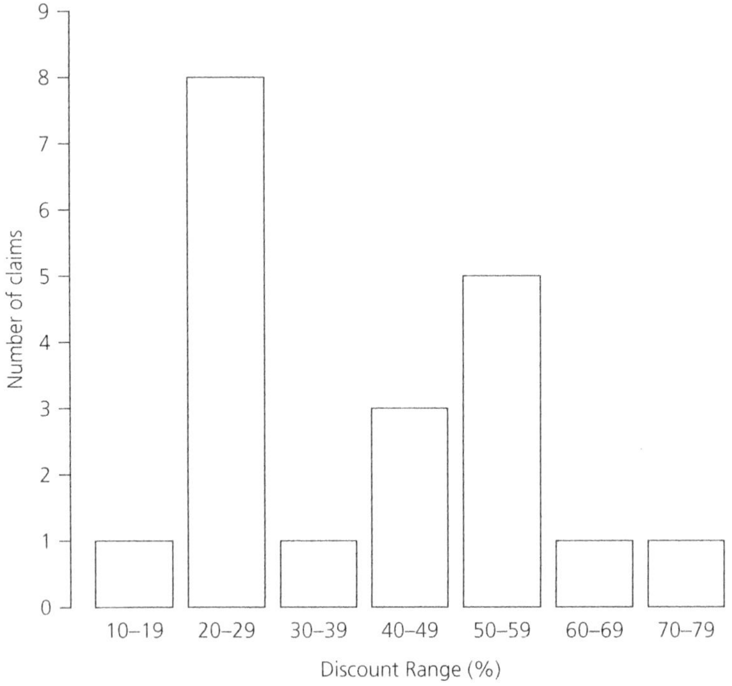

Figure 13.2 Number of claims by discount range

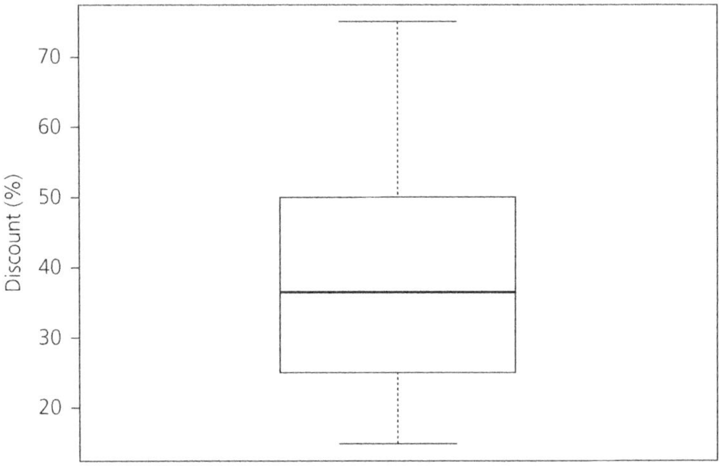

Figure 13.3 Boxplot of discounts

(3) Remarks Regarding the Statistics

The discounts in cases of this type exhibit quite a high degree of variability, as indicated by both the relatively large range (60%) and the standard deviation (16.7%). Nevertheless, in all but two claims, the discount was 50% or less. The average discount of 37.3% is not far off the average of 40% across all first instance claims. **13.02**

(4) Illustration of Case Involving a Discount Near the Average

In *Ellis v Bristol City Council*,[1] the claimant was employed by the defendant council to provide nursing care at a home for elderly and infirm persons. While working, the claimant slipped and fell in a pool of urine which had been left by one of the residents in the main corridor of the home. The floor was made from vinyl and slippery when wet. The claimant was found guilty of contributory negligence due to her failure to keep a proper lookout. The defendant had placed a warning sign regarding the slipping hazard in the staff room and near where the claimant fell. Non-slip mats had been placed in the vicinity but they did not cover the section of floor where the accident happened. A 33.3% discount was imposed. **13.03**

(5) Illustration of Case Involving a High Discount

In *McEwan v Lothian Buses Plc*,[2] the pursuer was an experienced motor mechanic who had been employed by the defender bus company. The pursuer was working alone at the relevant time in the defender's depot. In the course of the pursuer repairing the coolant system of a bus, which was a task that he had not previously undertaken, coolant leaked from the bus and flowed onto a board that was partially covering a pit. The pursuer suffered injury when he slipped on the board, which had become dangerous due to the presence of the coolant. The pursuer was found guilty of contributory negligence in spilling the coolant, failing to clean it up, and proceeding over the board when he had no reason to do so. The defender was held to have been negligent in failing to provide receptacles that would have caught some of the coolant, failing to provide cleaning equipment sufficient to deal with spillages, and failing to provide cleaning staff on the weekend, which is when the accident happened. A discount of 75% was imposed. **13.04**

[1] [2007] EWCA Civ 685, [2007] ICR 1614.
[2] 2006 SCLR 592 (OH).

(6) Illustration of Case Involving a Low Discount

13.05 In *Cheung v Zhu (t/a Yang Sing Fish & Chip)*,[3] the claimant, who was then aged 53, was employed by the defendant to work in her fish-and-chip shop. As the claimant was leaving work at the end of a long shift, she slipped on rainwater that had accumulated on the tiled floor of the defendant's premises and fell over. The rainwater had been able to accumulate on the floor as the door to the premises had been left open, and nothing had been laid on the floor to absorb the water. The claimant either knew or ought to have known that the floor was wet on the night in question. It was not the claimant's job to clean up the water. A 15% discount was imposed.

(7) Claims in the Sample for this Chapter

13.06 (1) *Cheung v Zhu (t/a Yang Sing Fish and Chip)* [2011] EWHC 2913 (QB) (15%); (2) *Caerphilly CBC v Button* [2010] EWCA Civ 1311, [2011] ICR D3 (20%); (3) *Campbell v Elliot Group Ltd* [2009] CSOH 63 (20%); (4) *Craigie v Lanarkshire Health Board* [2005] CSOH 118 (20%); (5) *Bailey v Command Security Services Ltd* 2001 WL 1535385 (QBD) (25%); (6) *Bailey v Command Security Services Ltd* 2001 WL 1535385 (QBD) (25%); (7) *Coates v Jaguar Cars Ltd* [2004] EWCA Civ 337 (25%); (8) *Parkinson v Northern Ireland Fire and Rescue Service* [2009] NIQB 87 (25%); (9) *James v H Buxton & Sons Ltd* 1999 WL 851957 (CA) (25%); (10) *Ellis v Bristol CC* [2007] EWCA Civ 685, [2007] ICR 1614 (33.3%); (11) *Johnstone v AMEC Constructions Ltd* [2010] CSIH 57 (40%); (12) *MacKenzie v Co-Operative Group (CWS) Ltd* 2007 Scot (D) 14/6 (Dingwall Sheriff Court) (40%); (13) *Wells v Mutchmeats Ltd* [2006] EWCA Civ 963 (40%); (14) *Anderson v Newham College for Further Education* [2002] EWCA Civ 505, [2003] ICR 212 (50%); (15) *Burgess v Plymouth CC* [2005] EWCA Civ 1659, [2006] ICR 579 (50%); (16) *Home Office v Lowles* [2004] EWCA Civ 985 (50%); (17) *King v Rco Support Services Ltd* [2001] ICR 608 (CA) (50%); (18) *Taylor v Wincanton Group Ltd* [2009] EWCA Civ 1581 (50%); (19) *Willows v Craggs (t/a Wellingore Garages)* [1999] CLY 2855 (Lincoln CC) (66.6%); (20) *McEwan v Lothian Buses Plc* 2006 SCLR 592 (OH) (75%).[4]

[3] [2011] EWHC 2913 (QB).

[4] As to why the same case appears more than once in this sample, see 7.03.

14

SLIP-AND-FALL ACCIDENT: PUBLIC PLACE

(1) Scope of this Chapter

This chapter concerns claims arising from slip-and-fall accidents that occurred in a public place. **14.01**

(2) Descriptive Statistics

Number of claims	12
Average discount	31.6%
Mode	25%
Highest discount	50%
Lowest discount	25%
Standard deviation	9.3%

Figure 14.1

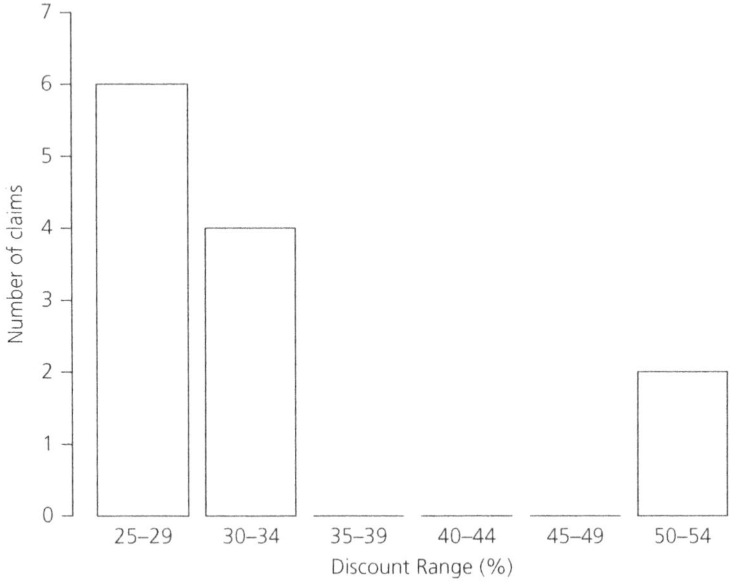

Figure 14.2 Number of claims by discount range

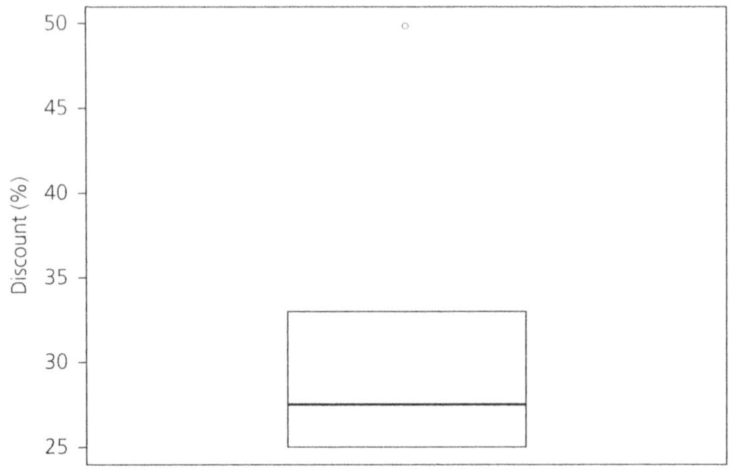

Figure 14.3 Boxplot of discounts

(3) Remarks Regarding the Statistics

14.02 The discounts in cases of this type exhibit a low degree of variability. The standard deviation is just 9.3% and, if the outlier is excluded from consideration, the range is modest at just 8%. In the claims sampled, therefore, the courts rarely imposed discounts that strayed far from the average.

The average discount of 31.6% is low relative to the average discount of 40% across first instance cases generally. In half of the claims, a discount of 25% was imposed, although relatively little can be made of this fact given that there are only 12 claims in this category. It is interesting to note that the average discount in this category of claims was somewhat lower than the average discount in claims involving a slip-and-fall accident that occurred in the workplace (37.3%).[1] **14.03**

(4) Illustration of Case Involving a Discount Near the Average

In *Walker v Newham LBC*,[2] the claimant had fallen and suffered injury when he placed his foot into a gap between two paving stones on a flight of steps outside his home. The gap had been present for at least eight or nine months prior to the accident and an employee of the defendant local authority who had inspected the steps prior to the accident had failed to notice it. The claimant knew of the danger (he passed up and down the steps approximately five times a week), had failed to report it to the defendant, and had fallen previously as a result of it. A 33.3% discount was imposed. **14.04**

(5) Illustration of Case Involving a High Discount

In *Maynard v Wigan MBC*,[3] the accident occurred on a grass verge outside the claimant's house. The claimant, who had been carrying her youngest child at the time, fell over when her foot entered a depression in the grass. The claimant had previously complained to the council about the depression, which was 'considerably more than 2 inches deep'.[4] A 50% discount was imposed. **14.05**

(6) Illustration of Case Involving a Low Discount

In *Dingley v Bromley LBC*,[5] the claimant had parked her car in a disabled space on a busy road. Upon exiting the vehicle, the claimant's foot entered a pothole in the parking space, causing her to fall and suffer injury. It was held that the defendant council had failed to put in place a proper system of inspection. The defendant had checked for potholes on Sunday mornings, when fewer vehicles were present. However, the court found that the defendant should have arranged for its inspectors to check for potholes hidden by parked cars. The claimant was **14.06**

---

[1] See 13.02.
[2] [2002] CLY 3256 (Central London CC).
[3] [2011] EWCA Civ 1694.
[4] ibid [29].
[5] [2000] CLY 4244 (Bromley CC).

held to be guilty of contributory negligence on the ground that she knew of the pothole's existence. A 25% discount was imposed.

(7) Claims in the Sample for this Chapter

14.07 (1) *Brown v City of Edinburgh Council* 1999 SLT (Sh Ct) 43 (Lothian and Borders Sheriff Court) (25%); (2) *Dingley v Bromley LBC* [2000] CLY 4244 (Bromley CC) (25%); (3) *Swain v Geoffrey Osborne Ltd* [2010] EWHC 1108 (QB) (25%); (4) *Swain v Geoffrey Osborne Ltd* [2010] EWHC 1108 (QB) (25%); (5) *Thorpe v Aberdeen CC* 2007 Rep LR 105 (Grampian, Highland and Islands Sheriff Court) (25%); (6) *Wilson v Glasgow CC* [2007] CSOH 143 (25%); (7) *Prentice v Hereward Housing Association Ltd* 1999 Lexis Citation 3165 (QBD) (30%); (8) *Bell v Havering LBC* [2010] EWCA Civ 689 (33.3%); (9) *Kemp v Secretary of State for Scotland* 2000 SLT 471 (OH) (33.3%); (10) *Walker v Newham LBC* [2002] CLY 3256 (Central London CC) (33.3%); (11) *Maynard v Wigan MBC* [2011] EWCA Civ 1694 (50%); (12) *Nixon v Thames Water Utilities Ltd* [2006] CLY 2913 (Romford CC) (50%).[6]

[6] As to why the same case appears more than once in this sample, see 7.03.

15

SLIP-AND-FALL ACCIDENT: OCCUPIERS' LIABILITY

(1) Scope of this Chapter

This chapter concerns claims arising out of slip-and-fall accidents where the defendant was sued as an occupier. 15.01

(2) Descriptive Statistics

Number of claims	14
Average discount	40.6%
Mode	20%, 50%, and 75%
Highest discount	75%
Lowest discount	10%
Standard deviation	22.5%

Figure 15.1

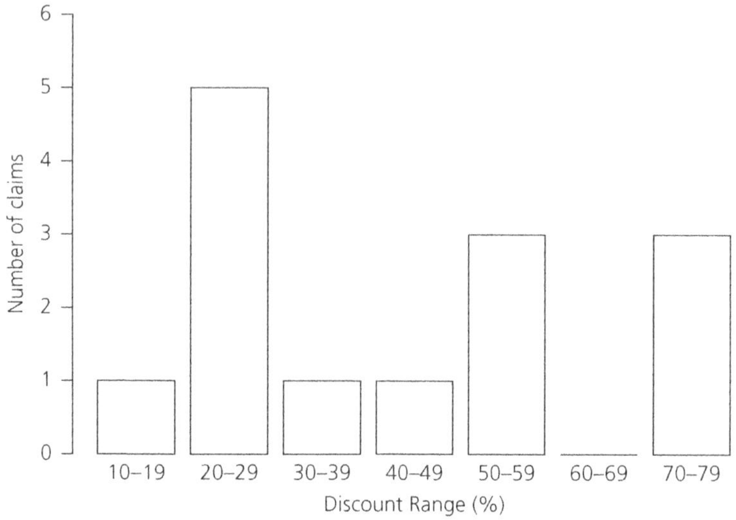

Figure 15.2 Number of claims by discount range

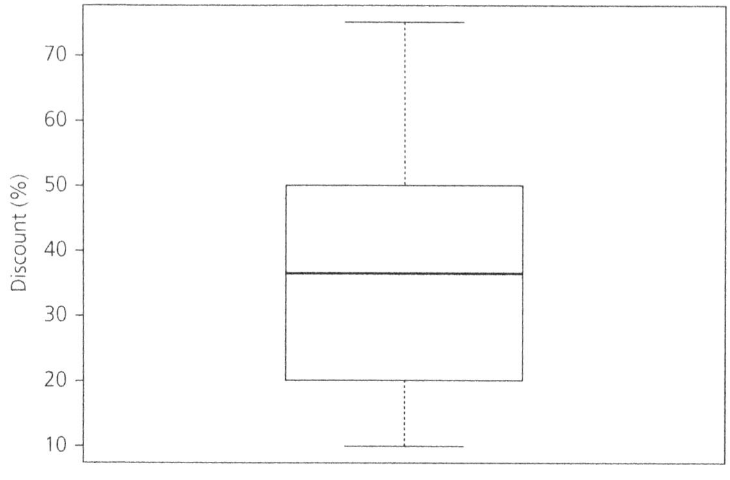

Figure 15.3 Boxplot of discounts

(3) Remarks Regarding the Statistics

15.02 The discounts in cases of this kind exhibit significant variability, as indicated by the relatively large standard deviation of 22.5%. The range of 65% is also substantial. Nonetheless, a discount of 50% or less was imposed in over three-quarters of claims.

15.03 The average discount of 40.6% is similar to the average discount of 40% across all first instance claims. It is higher than the average discounts imposed in the other two categories of slip-and-fall accidents, namely 37.3% (slip-and-fall accidents in the workplace[1]) and 31.6% (slip-and-fall accidents in public places[2]).

(4) Illustration of Case Involving a Discount Near the Average

A 33.3% discount was imposed in *Wells v Mutchmeats Ltd*.[3] The claimant was a meat inspector who had attended the first defendant's abattoir. A plastic tray had been placed by the first defendant in the doorway between two rooms within its premises. The tray was usually filled with disinfectant liquid, the weight of which would prevent the tray from moving when persons stepped into it. On the day in question, however, the tray was nearly empty. The claimant placed one of his feet into the tray and it slid away from him, causing him to fall and sustain injury. The trial judge held that the claimant was guilty of contributory negligence in stepping in the tray or, alternatively, in failing to move it. An appeal by the claimant to the Court of Appeal was dismissed. However, it was suggested in the Court of Appeal[4] that a lower discount might have been imposed had the matter been considered *de novo*. **15.04**

(5) Illustration of Case Involving a High Discount

In *Harvey v Plymouth CC*,[5] the claimant, who was 21 years old at the time of the accident, fell from one plot of land onto another. The height differential between the two plots was 5½ metres. The accident occurred at night-time and the claimant had been 'drinking fairly heavily at various bars'[6] beforehand. After fleeing from a taxi without paying the fare, the claimant had run through some bushes and tripped over a chain link fence, which had been pushed down to a height of about 14 inches, and then fallen down the sheer drop. A 75% discount was imposed. **15.05**

(6) Illustration of Case Involving a Low Discount

In *Lawson v The Broomfield Holiday Park*,[7] the pursuer was walking along a private road at a camping and caravan site after dark. She tripped over a speed hump and fell to the ground. The lighting provided was insufficient to allow pedestrians to see the speed hump in the dark. No signs warning of the hump had been **15.06**

1 See 13.02.
2 See 14.02.
3 [2006] EWCA Civ 963.
4 ibid [17] (Gage LJ), [19] (Moses LJ).
5 [2010] EWCA Civ 860, [2010] PIQR P18.
6 ibid [8].
7 2007 Scot (D) 9/7 (Dingwall Sheriff Court).

placed next to it, and a warning that had been written on the hump had not been painted in reflective paint. The pursuer was found guilty of contributory negligence on the basis that she was aware of the presence of two speed humps on the road in question, having driven along the road earlier in the day. Furthermore, the pursuer had also failed to take reasonable care for her own safety by not carrying a torch. A 20% discount was imposed.

(7) Claims in the Sample for this Chapter

15.07 (1) *Craig v Strathclyde Regional Council* 1998 Hous LR 104 (Sheriff Court) (10%); (2) *Lawson v The Broomfield Holiday Park* 2007 Scot (D) 9/7 (Dingwall Sheriff Court) (20%); (3) *Palfrey v VM Morrisons Supermarkets Plc* [2012] EWCA Civ 1917 (20%); (4) *Dean and Chapter of Rochester Cathedral v Debell* [2016] EWCA Civ 1094 (20%); (5) *Lawrence v NCL (Bahamas) Ltd (t/a Norwegian Cruise Line)* [2016] EWHC (Admlty) (25%); (6) *Morgan v Twyford Tots Nursery Ltd* [2006] CLY 2912 (Telford CC) (25%); (7) *Spencer v Wincanton Holdings Ltd* [2009] EWCA Civ 1404 (33.3%); (8) *Wells v Mutchmeats Ltd* [2006] EWCA Civ 963 (40%); (9); *Butcher v Southend-on-Sea BC* [2014] EWCA Civ 1556 (50%); (10) *Burgess v Plymouth CC* [2005] EWCA Civ 1659, [2006] ICR 579 (50%); (11) *English Heritage v Taylor* [2016] EWCA Civ 448 (50%); (12) *Buyukardicli v Hammerson UK Properties Plc* [2002] EWCA Civ 683 (75%); (13) *Buyukardicli v Hammerson UK Properties Plc* [2002] EWCA Civ 683 (75%); (14) *Harvey v Plymouth CC* [2010] EWCA Civ 860 (75%).[8]

[8] As to why the same case appears more than once in this sample, see 7.03.

16

CARELESSNESS IN CONNECTION WITH WORK EQUIPMENT

(1) Scope of this Chapter

This chapter concerns claims in which the claimant was found guilty of contributory negligence in the manner in which work equipment was used. It does not include claims where the claimant was working at height and injured in a fall, which are the subject of Chapter 17. **16.01**

(2) Descriptive Statistics

Number of claims	18
Average discount	37.7%
Mode	50%
Highest discount	70%
Lowest discount	15%
Standard deviation	15.4%

Figure 16.1

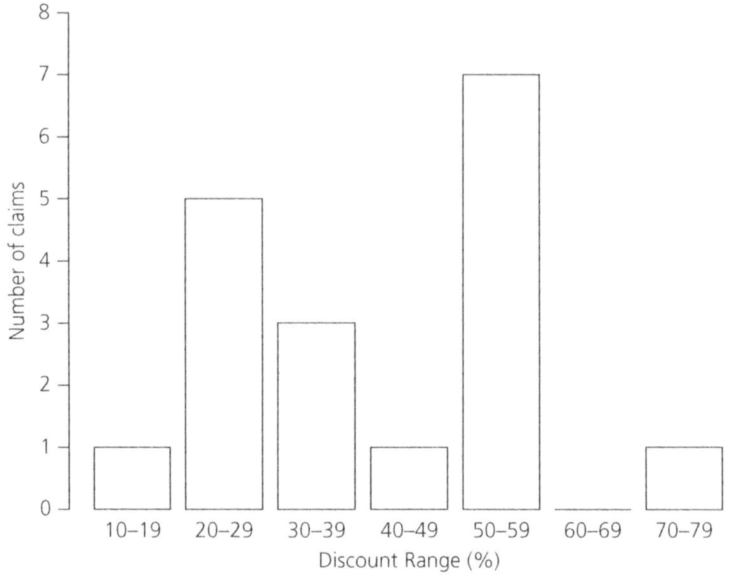

Figure 16.2 Number of claims by discount range

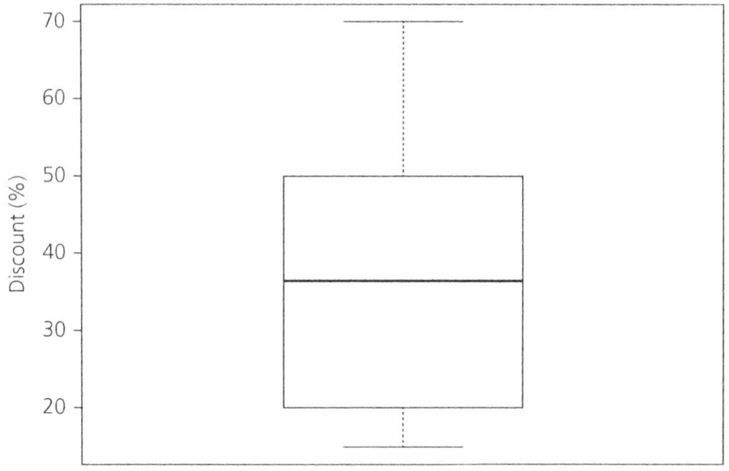

Figure 16.3 Boxplot of discounts

(3) Remarks Regarding the Statistics

16.02 The distribution of discounts is skewed towards the lower end of the spectrum. Fifty per cent was the most common discount by some margin, and there was only a single discount in excess of that figure. The average discount of 37.7% is marginally lower than the average discount of 40% across all first instance claims.

(4) Illustration of Case Involving a Discount Near the Average

In *Milroy v British Telecommunications Plc*,[1] the claimant engineer had been employed by the defendant to work on elevated mobile platforms. While working on a raised platform, the claimant came into contact with high-voltage powerlines and suffered serious injury. The defendant was found to have breached its common law duty of care and various statutory duties by giving the claimant inadequate training regarding the use of mobile platforms in the vicinity of high-voltage powerlines. The defendant was also held to be vicariously liable for the negligence of another of its employees, who had failed to consider a method of work that did not involve using the mobile platform in close proximity to the powerlines. The trial judge held, however, that the claimant had been guilty of contributory negligence in driving the mobile platform in a manner that led to the accident when he knew that the powerlines were nearby, and in failing to keep a proper lookout. Damages were reduced by 33.3%. **16.03**

(5) Illustration of Case Involving a High Discount

In *Woods v Police Service of Northern Ireland*,[2] the claimant police officer, who was employed as a senior armourer, accidentally shot himself in the hand while dismantling a gun. The gun concerned had been presented to him by another police officer as being defective. The claimant alleged that his employer had breached various statutory duties regarding the provision of safe work equipment. The claimant had extensive experience and training with guns, including in relation to the type of gun in issue. The trial judge held that the employer had wrongfully failed to ensure that a 'range officer' was present to check that the weapon was safe to handle. The claimant was found guilty of contributory negligence in various respects, including in firing the weapon before dismantling it, failing to point it in a safe direction, and failing to devise and follow a risk assessment in connection with the test firing and dismantling of the weapon. Damages were reduced by 50%. **16.04**

(6) Illustration of Case Involving a Low Discount

In *McLellan v Dundee CC*,[3] the pursuer was a gardener employed by the defender local authority. He was using a motorized lawnmower when the blades became clogged by wet grass. The pursuer used a crowbar, with which he had been supplied by the defender, to remove the grass. Once the grass had been removed, the **16.05**

---

[1] [2015] EWHC 532 (QB).
[2] [2009] NIQB 35.
[3] [2009] CSOH 9, 2009 Rep LR 61.

mower's blades started moving again even though the mower had been switched off, on account of energy that had been retained in the mower's hydraulic system. The pursuer's hand came into contact with the blades whereupon he suffered serious injury. In addition to acting negligently, the defender was found to have breached statutory duties that required it to conduct proper risk assessments and to provide the pursuer with adequate health and safety information about the operation of the mower. The pursuer had, however, also been at fault in putting his hand in close proximity to the blades while trying to clear the blockage, despite having been instructed to keep his hands well clear of the blades at all times. Damages were reduced by 20%.

(7) Claims in the Sample for this Chapter

16.06 (1) *Kern v Bridgend CBC* (Bridgend CC, 17 October 2008) (15%); (2) *Hyndman v Brown* [2012] NICA 3 (20%); (3) *McLellan v Dundee CC* [2009] CSOH 9, 2009 Rep LR 61 (20%); (4) *McLellan v Mitie Group Plc* [2015] CSOH 151, 2015 SLT 861 (20%); (5) *Sowmez v Kebaberry Wholesale Ltd* [2008] EWHC 3366 (QB) (20%); (6) *Drinnan v The Bone Group Ltd* 2005 SLT (Sh Ct) 119 (South Strathclyde, Dumfries and Galloway Sheriff Court) (25%); (7) *Causby v Seagoe Technologies Ltd* [2009] NIQB 24 (33.3%); (8) *Fraser v Winchester Health Authority* 1999 WL 477756 (CA) (33.3%); (9) *Milroy v British Telecommunications Plc* [2015] EWHC 532 (QB) (33.3%); (10) *Marsden v Ministry of Defence* (QBD, 11 November 1998) (40%): (11) *Ashbridge v Christian Salvesen Plc* [2006] CSOH 79, 2006 SLT 697 (50%); (12) *Chapman v Tangmere Airfield Nurseries Ltd* 1998 WL 1042616 (CA) (50%); (13) *Ellis v William Cook Leeds Ltd* [2007] EWCA Civ 1232 (50%); (14) *Griffiths v Vauxhall Motors Ltd* [2003] EWCA Civ 412 (50%); (15) *Mcfarlane v Scottish Borders Council* 2005 SLT 359 (IH) (50%); (16) *Robertson v Glasgow CC* [2007] CSOH 89 (50%); (17) *Woods v Police Service of Northern Ireland* [2009] NIQB 35 (50%); (18) *Cox v Superior Forklift Services Ltd* (CA, 18 December 1998) (70%).

17

CARELESSNESS IN OR WHILE WORKING AT HEIGHT

(1) Scope of this Chapter

This chapter concerns claims in which the claimant was injured in a fall from a height and was found guilty of contributory negligence either in working at height at all, or in the manner in which the claimant worked while at height. **17.01**

(2) Descriptive Statistics

Number of claims	15
Average discount	38.6%
Mode	50%
Highest discount	60%
Lowest discount	20%
Standard deviation	13.1%

Figure 17.1

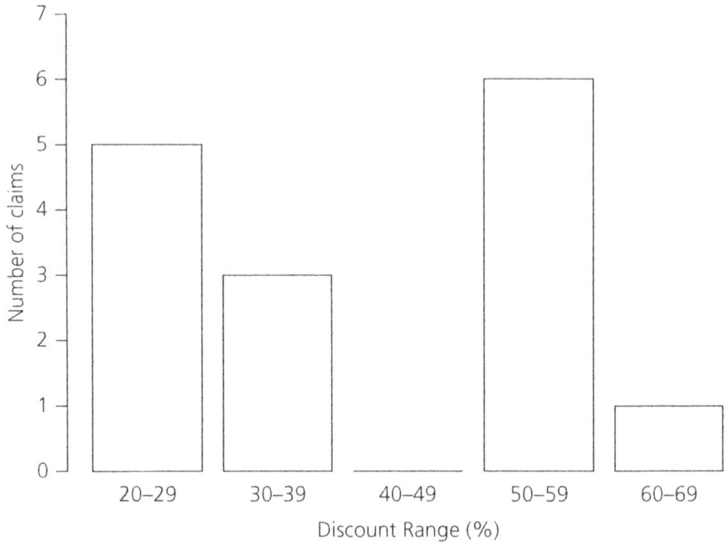

Figure 17.2 Number of claims by discount range

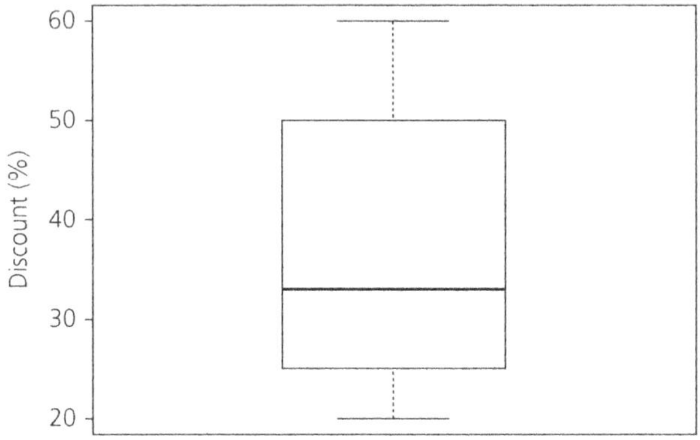

Figure 17.3 Boxplot of discounts

(3) Remarks Regarding the Statistics

17.02 All the discounts in this category of claims were below 60%, with 50% being the most popular discount, followed by 25%. Most claims fell between these last two figures. The relatively low variability of discounts is shown by the low standard deviation of 13.1%.

(4) Illustration of Case Involving a Discount Near the Average

In *Smith v Wilgar (t/a Wilgar Contracts)*,[1] the deceased fell from a 20ft ladder while working for the defendant employer. The deceased was a diabetic who had a history of suffering from hypoglycaemic attacks, a fact known to the defendant. It was common ground that the deceased had failed to control his diabetes. It was held that the defendant had breached statutory duties on account of its having failed to select appropriate equipment and in negligently failing to ensure a suitable system for work. Following a trial, it was determined that the claimant fell from the ladder as a result of a hypoglycaemic attack. Damages were reduced by 33.3% due to the claimant having failed to draw sufficiently clearly to the defendant's attention his history of such attacks. **17.03**

(5) Illustration of Case Involving a High Discount

In *Warke v British Telecommunications Plc*,[2] the claimant engineer was injured when a ladder that he was descending fell away from a telegraph pole on which he had been working. The claimant established that his employer had been guilty of negligence in failing to provide him with proper training in the use of ladders and had breached various statutory duties regarding the use of equipment in the workplace. The claimant was found to have been guilty of contributory negligence in failing to ensure that the stiles of the ladder were level before he ascended it and in failing to lash the bottom of the ladder to a nearby fence. Damages were reduced by 50%. **17.04**

(6) Illustration of Case Involving a Low Discount

In *Hill v Norside Ltd*,[3] the pursuer, a very experienced roofer, fell approximately 10ft while descending from scaffolding and broke his neck. The fall occurred when the ladder that the pursuer was using fell away from the scaffolding. The defender employer was found to have breached various statutory duties: it had failed to give any thought as to how its employees were to access the scaffolding and could easily have provided a safe system of work by installing a fixed ladder. **17.05**

---

1 [2011] NIQB 67.
2 [2004] NIQB 60.
3 [2012] CSOH 187, 2013 Rep LR 22.

However, the pursuer was contributorily negligent in failing to tie off the ladder. Damages were reduced by 20%. Lady Dorrian said:[4]

> For reasons relating to the much greater degree of control which they had over the site, and in particular, the scaffolding ... I consider that the blameworthiness of the defenders is of a very different degree to that of the pursuer. The fault of the defenders is not coextensive with that of the pursuer; it goes beyond, and is independent of it. The pursuer quite simply should not have been put in the position he was by the defenders. Inattention on the part of a workman is precisely one of the risks which the statutory duty is there to guard against.

(7) Claims in the Sample for this Chapter

17.06 (1) *Hill v Norside Ltd* [2012] CSOH 187, 2013 Rep LR 22 (20%); (2) *Gower-Smith v Hampshire CC* (Southampton CC, 27 June 2008) (25%); (3) *McLachlan v Early Learning Centre Ltd* [2011] CSOH 25, 2011 Rep LR 30 (25%); (4) *Donaldson v Brighton & Hove Council* 2001 WL 1743237 (Lewes CC) (25%); (5) *Donaldson v Brighton & Hove Council* 2001 WL 1743237 (Lewes CC) (25%); (6) *Bhatt v Fontain Motors Ltd* [2010] EWCA Civ 863, [2010] PIQR P17 (33.3%); (7) *Proctor v City Facilities Management Ltd* [2012] NIQB 99 (33.3%); (8) *Smith v Wilgar (t/a Wilgar Contracts)* [2011] NIQB 67 (33.3%); (9) *Leitch v Reid* [2003] NIQB 45 (50%); (10) *Neil v East Ayrshire Council* 2005 Rep LR 18 (OH) (50%); (11) *Robb v Salamis (M&I) Ltd* [2006] UKHL 56, [2007] ICR 175 (50%); (12) *Toner v George Morison Builders* [2010] CSOH 125, 2011 Rep LR 18 (50%); (13) *Warke v British Telecommunications Plc* [2004] NIQB 60 (50%); (14) *Wharf v Bildwell Insulations Ltd* [1999] CLY 2047 (QBD) (50%); (15) *Brown v Farmview Dairies Ltd* (QBD, 18 December 1998) (60%).[5]

[4] ibid [29].
[5] As to why the same case appears more than once in this sample, see 7.03.

18

CHILDREN INJURED WHILE PLAYING

(1) Scope of this Chapter

This chapter concerns claims in which a child suffered injury while playing. **18.01**

(2) Descriptive Statistics

Number of claims	11
Average discount	35.1%
Mode	25.5%
Highest discount	60%
Lowest discount	15%
Standard deviation	14.5%

Figure 18.1

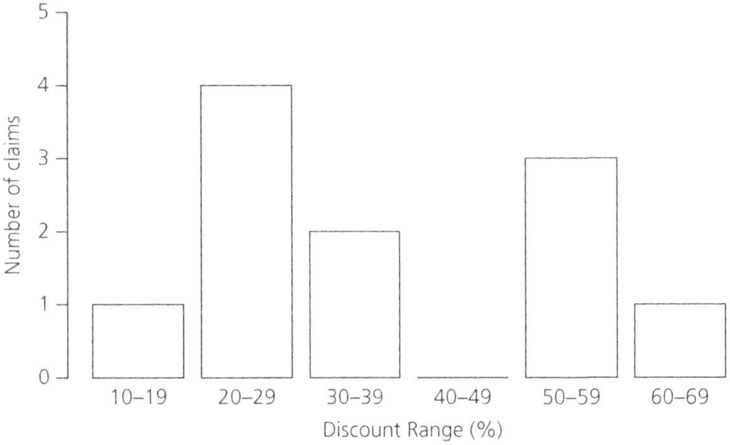

Figure 18.2 Number of claims by discount range

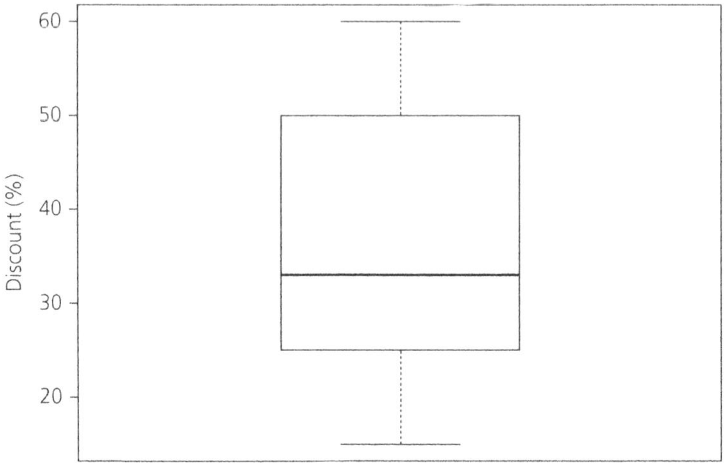

Figure 18.3 Boxplot of discounts

(3) Remarks Regarding the Statistics

18.02 The highest discount imposed in this category was 60%, and the average discount, 35%, was a little lower than the average in first instance claims generally (40%). Most of the discounts fell between 25% and 50%.

(4) Illustration of Case Involving a Discount Near the Average

18.03 In *DE v S Garages Ltd*,[1] the claimant, who was then aged 13 years (but a few days short of his fourteenth birthday), suffered serious burns when petrol with which he had been playing ignited. The claimant, together with a friend (also aged 13), had purchased the petrol from the defendant's garage and had been sniffing it. The trial judge found that the claimant's friend had thrown something down, whether a match or a cigarette, which caused the petrol to ignite. Damages were reduced by 33.3%. The judge said:

> [T]he defendants put the petrol into circulation when clearly they ought not to have. What happened, namely, ignition, was an obvious risk. The claimant knew that it was wrong for him to buy petrol and to sniff petrol, and that petrol was inflammable. I am not satisfied that he knew of its volatility. The claimant was at fault in acquiring the petrol. I am not satisfied that he turned his mind to the fact that anyone sniffing petrol might do something dangerous, nor do I think the reasonable 13-year-old would have thought in those terms. I accept ... the claimant's statement that he saw the sniffing as something which might raise a laugh. At the

[1] 2000 WL 33281292 (QBD).

same time, by the sniffing, which was a joint venture by the claimant and [his friend], they both became less responsible, which I suspect played some part in what happened.

(5) Illustration of Case Involving a High Discount

In *Young v Kent CC*,[2] the claimant, who was then aged 12½, was playing football unsupervised with friends at a school after school hours. The football ended up on the roof of one of the school's buildings. The claimant climbed onto the roof of the building concerned with a view to retrieving it but fell through a skylight and suffered serious injury. The defendant knew that children sometimes climbed onto the roof of the building in question, and that children had 'easy, ready access to the roof'[3] via a passageway. The defendant could have eliminated the danger by the 'low-cost solution'[4] of installing two short fences at either end of the passageway. The claimant 'ha[d] a complicated medical history with learning difficulties' and, the trial judge found, was thus 'more vulnerable than most other children to understanding the concepts of risk and danger'.[5] Damages were reduced by 50%. **18.04**

(6) Illustration of Case Involving a Low Discount

In *Re Kelly v Nugent*,[6] the claimant, who was aged nine years and eight months at the time of the accident, was playing on a tricycle. He cycled out onto a narrow country road whereupon he was hit by the defendant's vehicle. The trial judge found that the defendant had not kept a proper lookout, and had been driving too quickly, at around 20 mph, given the nature of the road. The claimant 'did acknowledge that whilst he had had no road traffic safety lessons in school until aged about 10 or 11, he did know it was dangerous to go out on to the road at this age and that his mother and father would not let him take his tricycle on to the road'. Damages were reduced by 15%. **18.05**

(7) Claims in the Sample for this Chapter

(1) *Re Kelly v Nugent* [2011] NIQB 79 (15%); (2) *McLeod v British Railways Board* 2001 SLT 238 (IH) (20%); (3) *Anderson v Imrie* [2016] CSOH 171, 2017 Rep LR 21 (25%); (4) *Jolley v Sutton LBC* [2000] 1 WLR 1082 (HL) (25%); (5) *Morton v Glasgow CC* 2007 SLT (Sh Ct) 81 (Glasgow and **18.06**

[2] [2005] EWHC 1342 (QB).
[3] ibid [33] (Morrison J).
[4] ibid.
[5] ibid [11].
[6] [2011] NIQB 79.

Strathkelvin Sheriff Court) (25%); (6) *Dawson v Scottish Power Plc* 1999 SLT 672 (OH) (33.3%); (7) *DE v S Garages Ltd* 2000 WL 33281292 (QBD) (33.3%); (8) *C v Imperial Design Ltd* [2001] Env LR 33 (CA) (50%); (9) *Wardle v Scottish Borders Council* 2011 SLT (Sh Ct) 199 (Lothian and Borders Sheriff Court) (50%); (10) *Young v Kent CC* [2005] EWHC 1342 (QB) (50%); (11) *N (a child) v Newham LBC* [2007] CLY 2931 (Central London CC) (60%).

19

OTHER RECURRENT SITUATIONS

We observed in the case law various other recurrent situations where the number of claims was lower than in the situations outlined in the chapters above. We have set out these recurrent situations below, along with the claims in the relevant category and the discounts imposed. We hope that this information will be useful to those faced with claims of the relevant kind in the future. However, we took the view that the numbers of claims in these categories were not high enough for statistical analysis to be illuminating. 19.01

Accepting ride from an intoxicated driver. (1) *W v Hardman* [2001] CLY 4452 (Leeds CC) (15%); (2) *Green v The Estate of Raymond Gaymer* 1999 WL 33232687 (QBD) (20%); (3) *Gleeson v Court* [2007] EWHC 2397 (QB), [2008] RTR 10 (30%); (4) *Currie v Clamp* 2002 SLT 196 (OH) (33.3%). 19.02

Unsafe overtaking. (1) *AC v TR* [2013] EWCA Civ 418, [2014] RTR 1 (50%); (2) *Woodham v M Turner (t/a Turners of Great Barton)* [2012] EWCA Civ 375 (50%); (3) *Moseley v Pell* [2003] EWCA Civ 1533 (50%); (4) *Ringe v Eden Springs (UK) Ltd* [2012] EWHC 14 (QB) (80%); (5) *Burton v Evitt* [2011] EWCA Civ 1378 (80%). 19.03

Failure to wear helmet. (1) *Perrin v Ministry of Defence* [2001] EWCA Civ 1310 (20%); (2) *McCracken v Smith* [2013] EWHC 3620 (QB) (45%); (3) *Reynolds v Strutt & Parker LLP* [2011] EWHC 2263 (QB) (66.6%). 19.04

Diving cases. (1) *McCarrick v Park Resorts Ltd* (QBD, 26 October 2012) (33.3%); (2) *Ministry of Defence v Radclyffe* [2009] EWCA Civ 635 (40%); (3) *Evans v Kosmar Villa Holiday Plc* [2007] EWCA Civ 1003, [2008] 1 WLR 297 (50%); (4) *Hurst v Thomson Holidays Ltd* [2004] CLY 1879 (Cambridge CC) (50%); (5) *Donoghue v Folkestone Properties Ltd* [2003] EWCA Civ 231 (75%). 19.05

Smoking (asbestos exposure cases). (1) *Shortell v BICAL Construction Ltd* (QBD, 16 May 2008) (15%); (2) *Badger v Ministry of Defence* [2005] EWHC 2941 (QB), [2006] 3 All ER 173 (20%); (3) *Horsley v Cascade Insulation Services Ltd* [2009] EWHC 2945 (QB) (20%); (4) *Horsley v Cascade Insulation Services Ltd* [2009] EWHC 2945 (QB) (20%); (5) *Blackmore v Department for Communities and Local Government* [2017] EWCA Civ 1136, [2018] PIQR P1 (30%). 19.06

Dangerous lifting. (1) *Goodchild v Organon Laboratories Ltd* [2004] EWHC 2341 (QB) (10%); (2) *Tibbatts v British Airways Plc* [2009] EWHC 815 (QB) 19.07

(33.3%); (3) *Costa v Imperial London Hotels Ltd* [2012] EWCA Civ 672 (35%); (4) *Quinn v Keenan* [2013] NIQB 55 (50%); (5) *Egan v Central Manchester and Manchester Children's University Hospital NHS Trust* [2008] EWCA Civ 1424, [2009] ICR 585 (50%); (6) *Lips v Older* [2004] EWHC 1686 (QB), [2005] PIQR P14 (66.6%).

APPENDIX 1

Law Reform (Contributory Negligence) Act 1945

An Act to amend the law relating to contributory negligence and for purposes connected therewith.

1. Apportionment of liability in case of contributory negligence

(1) Where any person suffers damage as the result partly of his own fault and partly of the fault of any other person or persons, a claim in respect of that damage shall not be defeated by reason of the fault of the person suffering the damage, but the damages recoverable in respect thereof shall be reduced to such extent as the court thinks just and equitable having regard to the claimant's share in the responsibility for the damage:

Provided that—

(a) this subsection shall not operate to defeat any defence arising under a contract;
(b) where any contract or enactment providing for the limitation of liability is applicable to the claim, the amount of damages recoverable by the claimant by virtue of this subsection shall not exceed the maximum limit so applicable.

(2) Where damages are recoverable by any person by virtue of the foregoing subsection subject to such reduction as is therein mentioned, the court shall find and record the total damages which would have been recoverable if the claimant had not been at fault.

(3) ...

(4) ...

(5) Where, in any case to which subsection (1) of this section applies, one of the persons at fault avoids liability to any other such person or his personal representative by pleading the Limitation Act 1939, or any other enactment limiting the time within which proceedings may be taken, he shall not be entitled to recover any damages from that other person or representative by virtue of the said subsection.[1]

(6) Where any case to which subsection (1) of this section applies is tried with a jury, the jury shall determine the total damages which would have been recoverable if the claimant had not been at fault and the extent to which those damages are to be reduced.

(7) ...

[1] In the case of Scotland, subsection 1(5) provides: 'Where, in any case to which subsection (1) of this section applies, one of the persons at fault avoids liability to any other such person or his personal representative by pleading the Limitation Act 1939, or any other enactment limiting the time within which proceedings may be taken, he shall not be entitled to recover any damages or contributions from that other person or representative by virtue of the said subsection.'

2. ...

3. Saving for Maritime Conventions Act 1911, and past cases

(1) This Act shall not apply to any claim to which section one of the Maritime Conventions Act, 1911, applies and that Act shall have effect as if this Act had not passed.
(2) This Act shall not apply to any case where the acts or omissions giving rise to the claim occurred before the passing of this Act.

4. Interpretation

The following expressions have the meanings hereby respectively assigned to them, that is to say—

'court' means, in relation to any claim, the court or arbitrator by or before whom the claim falls to be determined;
'damage' includes loss of life and personal injury;
...
'fault' means negligence, breach of statutory duty or other act or omission which gives rise to a liability in tort or would, apart from this Act, give rise to the defence of contributory negligence.

5. Application to Scotland

In the application of this Act to Scotland—

(a) the expression *'dependant'* means, in relation to any person, any person who would in the event of such first mentioned person's death through the fault of a third party be entitled to sue that third party for damages or solatium; and the expression *'fault'* means wrongful act, breach of statutory duty or negligent act or omission which gives rise to liability in damages, or would apart from this Act, give rise to the defence of contributory negligence;
(b) section 3 of the Law Reform (Miscellaneous Provisions) (Scotland) Act 1940 (contribution among joint wrongdoers) shall apply in any case where two or more persons are liable, or would if they had all been sued be liable, by virtue of section 1(1) of this Act in respect of the damage suffered by any person.
(c) for subsection (4) of section one the following subsection shall be substituted—
'(4) Where any person dies as the result partly of his own fault and partly of the fault of any other person or persons, a claim by any dependant of the first mentioned person for damages or solatium in respect of that person's death shall not be defeated by reason of his fault, but the damages or solatium recoverable shall be reduced to such extent as the court thinks just and equitable having regard to the share of the said person in the responsibility for his death.'

6. Provisions as to Northern Ireland

(1) ...
(2) This Act shall not extend to Northern Ireland.

7. Short title and extent.

This Act may be cited as the Law Reform (Contributory Negligence) Act 1945.

APPENDIX 2

Law Reform (Miscellaneous Provisions) Act (Northern Ireland) 1948

An Act to abolish the defence of common employment; to amend the law relating to contributory negligence and the measure of damages for personal injury or death; and for purposes connected with the matters aforesaid.

. . .

2. Apportionment of liability in tort where more than one person is at fault

(1) Where any person suffers damage as the result partly of his own fault and partly of the fault of any other person or persons, a claim in respect of that damage shall not be defeated by reason of the fault of the person suffering the damage, but the damages recoverable in respect thereof shall be reduced to such extent as the court thinks just and equitable having regard to the claimant's share in the responsibility for the damage:

Provided that—

(a) this sub-section shall not operate to defeat any defence arising under a contract;

(b) where any contract or enactment providing for the limitation of liability is applicable to the claim, the amount of damages recoverable by the claimant by virtue of this sub-section shall not exceed the maximum limit so applicable.

. . .

(2) Where damages are recoverable by any person by virtue of the preceding sub-section subject to such reduction as is therein mentioned, the court shall find and record the total damages which would have been recoverable if the claimant had not been at fault.

(5) Where, in any case to which sub-section (1) of this section applies, one of the persons at fault or his personal representative avoids liability to any other such person or his personal representative by pleading any enactment limiting the time within which proceedings may be taken, he shall not be entitled to recover any damages . . . from that other person or representative by virtue of the said sub-section.

(6) Where any case to which sub-section (1) of this section applies is tried with a jury, the jury shall determine the total damages which would have been recoverable if the claimant had not been at fault and the extent to which those damages are to be reduced.

. . .

4. Operation of Act and saving for Maritime Conventions Act, 1911

(1) Sections one, two and sub-section (1) of section three of this Act shall apply only where the cause of action accrues after the passing of this Act; but sub-sections (4) and (5) of the said section three shall apply whether the cause of action accrued or the proceedings were commenced before or after such passing.

(2) Section two of this Act shall not apply to any case to which section 187 of the Merchant Shipping Act 1995, applies.

5. Application to Crown

(1) Sections one and three of this Act shall bind the Crown as from the day on which the Crown Proceedings Act, 1947, is, by virtue of an Order in Council made under section fifty-three of the last-mentioned Act, extended to Northern Ireland.

(2) So much of sections four and six of this Act as relates to the said sections one and three shall bind the Crown as from the day referred to in the preceding sub-section, so, however, that in relation to proceedings against the Crown the references in sub-section (1) of the said section four to the passing of this Act shall be construed as references to the said day.

6. Interpretation

(1) In this Act the following expressions have the meanings hereby respectively assigned to them, that is to say—

'court' means, in relation to any claim, the court or arbitrator by or before whom the claim falls to be determined;

'damage' includes loss of life and personal injury;

'fault' means negligence, breach of statutory duty or other act or omission which gives rise to a liability in tort or would, but for this Act, give rise to the defence of contributory negligence;

'personal injury' includes any disease and any impairment of a person's physical or mental condition, and the expression 'injured' shall be construed accordingly.

7. Short title

This Act may be cited as the Law Reform (Miscellaneous Provisions) Act (Northern Ireland), 1948.

INDEX

Made in the USA
Monee, IL
08 November 2026

68172871R00089